Bible Prophecy Made Simple For Serious Students of Scripture

James Battell

Published by James Battell, 2024.

BIBLE PROPHECY MADE SIMPLE FOR SERIOUS STUDENTS OF SCRIPTURE

First edition. January 31, 2024.

Copyright © 2024 James Battell.

ISBN: 979-8230313472

Written by James Battell.

Also by James Battell

The Shocking History of the Jesuits (The Society of Jesus)
King James I of England: The King The Vatican Could Not Kill
The Hidden Truth About Freemasonry, The Catholic Church, And The Illuminati
Bible Prophecy Made Simple For Serious Students of Scripture
Did The Catholic Church Order Abraham Lincoln's Assassination?
Is Calvinism and the Doctrines of Grace Biblical?
The Book of Genesis Commentary (Chapters 1-11)
The Book of Genesis Commentary (Chapters 1-11)
Watchman Nee, Witness Lee, and Living Stream Ministry: A Critical Analysis of Their Identity as Cult or Church
What Is Speaking In Tongues And Is It Still For Today?
Ephesians KJV Bible Commentary
The Book of Romans Commentary
Philemon Bible Study (Slavery In Scripture)
Turbulent Thrones: Charles vs. Cromwell's Epic Struggle for England's Soul
The Holy Ghost Within The Trinity
Papal Infallibility or Insanity?
The Immaculate Conception ("Deception")

Table of Contents

Matthew 24

Revelation 1

Daniel 12

Isaiah 66

Daniel 9

I don't know how long this series is going to last. I'm currently going through the Scriptures. I read the Bible every day, and it's something which all Christians should be doing. And I want to look at the subject of eschatology. Eschatology is a very important subject, and if the truth be known, most churches have no interest in the second coming of Christ. Most churches are post-millennial, and for those that don't know, post-millennialism simply means the idea, the notion that if all of the churches can work together, they can bring in the Kingdom of God. And you would have thought after a couple of world wars, after two Iraq wars, Vietnam, Ireland (the troubles), Afghanistan, and all the other wars that have been going on since the beginning of the 20th century, such a notion would have been lost. But, sadly, it's still held by many, many people.

Matthew 24 is one of the most important parts of Scripture when it comes to how the last days are going to play out. There is a difference between "the last days" and "the latter days," and normally when the Bible says "the last days," it can refer to positionally in the sense that Jesus was sent to the people of Israel and He was their last prophet, if you will, and what He said had overall importance to everything that has gone before it. If we look at Hebrews Chapter 1, it says here: "God, who at sundry times and in divers manners spake in time past unto the fathers by the prophets, Hath in these last days spoken unto us by his Son, whom he hath appointed heir of all things, by whom also he made the worlds." So that reference "the last days" can refer to Christ Himself coming as the Messiah, of course, of Israel.

But if we go to 1 Timothy, we also find that the expression "latter times" also has still a future timeframe. Look at verse 1, 1 Timothy 4:1:

2

"Now the Spirit speaketh expressly, that in the latter times some shall depart from the faith, giving heed to seducing spirits, and doctrines of devils; Speaking lies in hypocrisy; having their conscience seared with a hot iron; Forbidding to marry, and commanding to abstain from meats, which God hath created to be received with thanksgiving of them which believe and know the truth." And I'll let you search your own history books as to which religion bans marriage between a man and a woman and which religion wouldn't allow meat to be consumed on a Friday, and if you know your history, you'll know who I'm referring to. So there you are: Two different expressions – latter times and the last times or the last day.

So Matthew 24, Jesus is speaking to His Jewish apostle. It's always important to get the context right. And I'm just going to skim through these verses. There's no way I can read them all. I'll be here forever if I do.

MATTHEW 24

VERSE 1: "And Jesus went out, and departed from the temple: and his disciples came to him for to shew him the buildings of the temple."

He must have seen this building thousands of times, and yet this would be the last time that they would see it in its complete glory. Of course, you had 40 years before it was obliterated, but for the Lord Jesus, this would be the last time He would see it.

VERSE 2: "And Jesus said unto them, See ye not all these things? verily I say unto you, There shall not be left here one stone upon another, that shall not be thrown down."

Of course, that is a reference to the destruction 40 years later. And we know a lot of the Jews were starved to death. It was a horrific period, and Josephus is quite vocal about this period of time. If you want to read his own account of it, it goes into much more detail.

Also, something just to add before I go on. You go to Jerusalem today and you see the Wailing Wall, and Jews and Gentiles will go there and put on their skullcap and sometimes rock sideways or backwards and forwards and leave their prayers in the wall. They fill out little cards and stuff them in the wall. At the end of the day, those notes are taken out and burnt, and they don't want too much litter cluttering that part of the Holy Wall. But for the Christians, we don't need to go to a wall and pray. We can go to Jesus Christ. Paul says in Ephesians, I think it is, that Christ has knocked down the middle wall of partition. We go straight to the Lord God through Christ Jesus. In fact, even Luther said that it wasn't necessary to go to the Holy Land to see the Lord. Just go to the epistles and you'll find Him there.

VERSE 3: "And as he sat upon the mount of Olives, the disciples came unto him privately, saying, Tell us, when shall these things be? and what shall be the sign of thy coming, and of the end of the world?"

Three questions are asked of Him: When will these things be? What will be the sign of your coming and the end of the world? Now, only Matthew's Gospel gives you those three questions.

VERSE 4: "And Jesus answered and said unto them, Take heed that no man deceive you."

And, of course, many people are being deceived today and have been deceived since this Gospel was written.

VERSE 5: "For many shall come in my name, saying, I am Christ; and shall deceive many."

When I read that, the first group of people that come to my mind are the popes of Rome. In total, the Catholic church would have you believe that they have produced 265 popes. My own research would severely question that number. A lot of these popes, if you want to call them popes, were rich people who bought the papacy and sat on the throne of Peter. We've had children on the throne; we've had insane people on the throne, murderers on the throne; we've even had more than one person on the throne at any given time. And according to many sources, even Pope Joan from England was on the throne back in the 12th century, I believe. And we've spoken about her in our newsletter, which you may want to read. And just a quick footnote also, there's a film that's just been made about Joan, and apparently this woman fell pregnant and was killed by the church of Rome. So there you are.

Look at verse 8: **"All these are the beginning of sorrows."**

When we look at eschatology, we see it in two parts: The beginning of sorrows, which feeds into the Great Tribulation, and we do believe at this ministry that the Great Tribulation and the beginning of sorrows will be seven years, two three-and-a-half year periods apiece. And we look at Daniel's 70th week and Jacob's trouble, and I am convinced that Matthew 24, at least 90 percent of Matthew 24 is aimed at the Jews.

Look at verse 11: **"And many false prophets shall rise, and shall deceive many."**

There's your Benny Hinns, your Kenneth Copelands, your Joyce Meyers, your Todd Bentleys, Joel Osteens, Kenneth Hagin, Kenneth Copeland. All the people that are on television and on the radio, all the people that want your money are spoken of in verse 11. It's also fair to say that Hindus, Sikhs, Jews, Buddhists, the Freemasons, Bilderbergers – they'd also be classed as false prophets. But Christ is speaking about people who are claiming to come in His name – cross reference that, of course, with verse 5. During this time there will be great iniquity.

VERSE 12: "And because iniquity shall abound, the love of many shall wax cold."

A lot of people in the UK are cold; they're lukewarm, and because they're cold and lukewarm, they have no discernment. And when you tell them about some of these heretics, some of these charlatans, they just don't want to hear it.

VERSE 13: "But he that shall endure unto the end, the same shall be saved."

This form of endurance is in reference to the apostasy during this period of time, and you're told to endure the apostasy, to remain faithful to be saved from the apostasy. There are some good people, good dispensationalists who believe verse 13 is a reference to keeping the law during the Great Tribulation in order to be saved, and that, of course, is totally impossible.

I've also said previously that such views would normally be found in Catholic circles, and we need to be careful here because we are not able to save ourselves. We don't become junior partners with Christ in our atonement. The Catholic church would refer to this thinking as infused righteousness, which means, in essence, that God infuses some of His goodness to you – normally at baptism – and you continue on until you die. And, again, that puts you in a position as a junior partner with Christ, whereas the correct and historical view would be imputed righteousness. When a man or a woman cries out to the Lord, He gives them His own righteousness. And I don't believe in many different gospels for different dispensations. It's a very confusing theory, a system of theology which I don't believe the Bible supports.

VERSE 14: "And this gospel of the kingdom shall be preached in all the world for a witness unto all nations; and then shall the end come."

This also is referenced by some dispensationalists to refer to another Gospel, where Paul says in Galatians 1 if you preach any other Gospel, even if it comes from an angel, let him be accursed. We need to be so careful that we don't fall into the trap of becoming blinded by the simplicity which is in Jesus Christ. And another reference which is cited would be Revelation 14:6: **"And I saw another angel fly in the midst of heaven, having the everlasting gospel."** Well, "everlasting" means without end, from beginning to end, but everlasting, as I say, has no beginning and has no end. And it says there **"to preach unto them that dwell on the earth, and to every nation, and kindred, and tongue, and people, Saying with a loud voice, Fear God, and give glory to him; for the hour of his judgment is come: and worship him that made heaven, and earth, and the sea, and the fountains of waters."**

So you're told to fear God, to give glory to Him, for the hour of His judgment is come. That really is the Gospel which would be preached today – to fear God. To fear God means to believe in God, and to believe in God would mean to believe in Jesus Christ, because Jesus Christ is God, and give glory to Him, for the hour of His judgment is come. So I don't read Matthew 24:14 and Revelation 14:6 and 7 to be any other different Gospel to that found in Romans 10, Acts 16, and even in John 5:24. There's only one Gospel, and that is to believe on the Lord Jesus Christ, and then you will be saved.

VERSE 15: "When ye therefore shall see the abomination of desolation, spoken of by Daniel the prophet, stand in the holy place, (whoso readeth, let him understand:)"

Now, Daniel is a Jew writing to the Jews, and Jesus is a Jew speaking to the Jews, and in 30 AD all they had was the Temple in Jerusalem. The synagogues later became churches, and the Christian in 1 Corinthians 6 became a temple of the Holy Spirit. But that's not what's being spoken about here. The Antichrist, the man of sin, will go into the Temple and desecrate it like you find from Daniel's account.

VERSE 16: "Then let them which be in Judaea flee into the mountains:"

Not London, Paris, or Rome but Judaea. Again, Christ is speaking to the Jews in Israel.

VERSE 17: "Let him which is on the housetop not come down to take any thing out of his house:"

Acts 10 Peter prays. He goes into a trance, and he's praying on the top of his house, on the roof of his house. In the UK most houses are not flat; they are pointed, so you wouldn't be very comfortable to sit on a UK roof. I think it's the same in America too. But in first century Israel – and I've been there – a lot of the houses were flat.

VERSES 18-20: "Neither let him which is in the field return back to take his clothes. And woe unto them that are with child, and to them that give suck in those days! But pray ye that your flight be not in the winter, neither on the sabbath day:"

Again, the Sabbath is a Jewish feast day, civil and ceremonial, which, yes, is found in the Ten Commandments, but it is nonetheless a civil and ceremonial day given to the Jews under the law, which, according to Luke 24, was mandatory; you had to keep it, whereas in Romans 14 and Colossians 2, it's not mandatory. Paul says if you want to keep it, you can keep it, and if you don't, you don't. Christ is the Lord of the Sabbath, and He is our Sabbath rest according to Hebrews Chapter 4.

VERSE 21: "For then shall be great tribulation, such as was not since the **beginning of the world to this time, no, nor ever shall be.**"

This is a one-off event never seen and never to be experienced again. And I remember listening to – I think it was Billy Graham giving a talk to some Eastern Europeans years ago, and I think he was referencing the Holocaust, and he said at the time, "May this evil, this wickedness never happen again." Well, the Bible says, Billy, it's going to get even worse in the last days. But, of course, Graham doesn't believe that and, like a lot of apostates, simply goes with the flow.

VERSE 22: "And except those days should be shortened, there should no flesh be saved: but for the elect's sake those days shall be shortened."

Okay. Those that are going to be saved and for their sake only the days are limited.

VERSES 23-24: "Then if any man shall say unto you, Lo, here is Christ, or there; believe it not. For there shall arise false Christs, and false prophets, and shall shew great signs and wonders; insomuch that, if it were possible, they shall deceive the very elect."

It isn't possible, according to this. And these false prophets are going to show some real signs and wonders. Never mind the Benny Hinns and the Kenneth Copelands and the popes of today, but in the Tribulation these guys are going to be really powerful and they're going to be out to deceive on a large unprecedented scale.

VERSE 25: "Behold, I have told you before."

So you're now accountable. Jesus Christ has told you what's going to happen, and you could have known this. And if you live in a country in the West where they have the Internet in the library – and in the UK it's free – then you are without excuse. And if you are near to books and publications and tracts and pamphlets, you have no reason to be ignorant, and God will judge you as to what you could have known had you made the effort to know – not what you did know but what you could have known. That, of course, is a reference to unsaved people. If you're saved, then you're going to be judged by what you did know, of course, not just what you could have known; but if you are not saved, you will be judged by what you could have known but chose not to.

VERSES 26-28: "Wherefore if they shall say unto you, Behold, he is in the desert; go not forth: behold, he is in the secret chambers; believe it not. For as the lightning cometh out of the east, and shineth even unto the west; so shall also the coming of the Son of man be. For wheresoever the carcase is, there will the eagles be gathered together."

As the lightning strikes from the east to the west and we all see it, He's saying that so will it appear the sign of the Son of man coming. In other words, you won't miss Him. He'll be in the sky coming down, and wherever you are on planet earth, you will see His physical return at the end of the Tribulation to rule the world.

VERSE 29: "Immediately after the tribulation of those days shall the sun be darkened, and the moon shall not give her light, and the stars shall fall from heaven, and the powers of the heavens shall be shaken:"

These are not literal 24-hour days. They would be a reference to years. The stars which fall from Heaven would be a reference to angels, fallen angels, which Revelation also talks about.

VERSE 30: "And then shall appear the sign of the Son of man in heaven: and then shall all the tribes of the earth mourn, and they shall see the Son of man coming in the clouds of heaven with power and great glory."

Like I said, everybody is going to see Him coming, whether you believe in Him or not.

VERSE 31: "And he shall send his angels with a great sound of a trumpet, and they shall gather together his elect from the four winds, from one end of heaven to the other."

This is not a reference to a Rapture. This is a reference to the gathering together of those that are on earth to go up to meet Jesus in Jerusalem, Matthew 25, where you have the sheep and the goats.

VERSE 34: "Verily I say unto you, This generation shall not pass, till all these things be fulfilled."

This expression **"this generation"** has been argued and bickered over for many, many years. The way I look at it is the generation that He is referring to that are going to experience all of this will not pass until everything is fulfilled, not the generation He's speaking to because all these things didn't come to pass in His generation. He is speaking about a future generation.

VERSE 36: "But of that day and hour knoweth no man, no, not the angels of heaven, but my Father only."

Now, remember, Christ has two natures – the Son of man and the Son of God. As the Son of man, He was limited in scope; as the Son of God, obviously He was from eternity. The JWs will read this and say, "Well, there you are. He's just a good man, nothing more than that." No. That's not what He means. He said only the Father knows at that moment of time, and, of course, Christ is back in glory now, so He knows everything anyway. But also remember, while He was on the earth, He does say in John 10:30, "My Father and I are one." So He's not saying He's less than the Father. In fact, they're very much the same.

VERSES 40-41: "Then shall two be in the field; the one shall be taken, and the other left. Two women shall be grinding at the mill; the one shall be taken, and the other left."

Again, this is a reference to the angels gathering together those that are His on the earth at the end of the Tribulation and taking them to be with the Lord. Those that are left will have to wait for their own chance, their own time to stand before the Lord. And Matthew 13 also speaks about the wheat and the tares being separated and so on and so forth.

VERSES 48-51: "But and if that evil servant shall say in his heart, My lord delayeth his coming; And shall begin to smite his fellowservants, and to eat and drink with the drunken; The lord of that servant shall come in a day when he looketh not for him, and in an hour that he is not aware of, And shall cut him asunder, and

appoint him his portion with the hypocrites: there shall be weeping and gnashing of teeth."

Now, here's a picture of a man who wasn't saved – again, a tare, an unregenerate sinner who was considered to be a saved person by those around him, but his outcome is quite clearly evident that he was never saved to begin with.

I just want to do a recap on the previous two videos. We've looked at the main verses dealing with the subject of eschatology; and, like I said, Matthew 24 has a dual application. It is speaking first and foremost of the destruction of the Temple in 70 AD, but it has a much wider significance to the Great Tribulation. And a lot of Preterists – and they are the ones who believe that everything that Matthew 24 mentioned has already come to pass – and a lot of Preterists stumble with the greater significance of Matthew 24 and especially Romans 11, which shows that the Lord has not finished with the nation of Israel, per se.

I also spoke briefly about post-millennialism, and those that are post-millennial are trying to bring in the Kingdom of God on this earth without Christ on the throne, and that won't work. Only Christ Himself is able to initiate His thousand-year reign. And it is a fact that most churches in this country do not believe in a thousand-year reign pre-millennialism but are post-millennial and also a-millennial, and, of course, a-millennial means there is no Millennium. And we are very keen and eager to preach pre-millennialism, pre-mill for short.

Okay. We looked at, like I say, the main verses in Matthew 24, and we finished on verse 48, which speaks of that evil servant. Now, like all people in the Scriptures, you're either saved or you're not. This guy ends up being cut to pieces with the hypocrites and goes into Hell. My feeling on that account is that this man was never saved in the first place. Also, just a quick side point to flag up. This whole subject of servants and slaves, the word "slave" appears in your new Bibles. I think it was Westcott and Hort that translated "servant" into "slave." And, of course, a slave is a person with absolutely nothing to offer his master, if you will, whereas a servant has a bit more of a respectable connotation to it. But if you go to Galatians 4 and look at verse 7: **"Wherefore thou art no more a servant, but a son; and if a son, then an heir of God through Christ."** So the Christian is elevated from a servant to a son of God, an heir, a co-heir with Christ.

So I just want to get these terms right because a lot of people read the Gospels and never progress into the epistles. Most of the content in the Gospels are for the Jews under the law. A lot of Scripture tells the Jew to keep the Sabbath, keep the commandments, go to the Temple, do this and do that – it's all works-based under the Old Testament set up. As we've said before, all of the Bible is to us but it's not all for us. And that was a term coined by the late Dr. J. Vernon McGee, and it's absolutely right. Parts of the Scriptures are aimed doctrinally and primarily at the Jews, the Jews under the Old Testament, and we are saved men and women, according to Galatians 3, and we are no more Jew nor Greek, bond nor free, male nor female. We are all one in Christ Jesus. That means positionally when the Lord sees us, He sees us all as one person in Christ. Practically day by day, those roles can fluctuate. Not all men are called to be Bible teachers, missionaries, evangelists, so on and so forth; and women aren't called to be pastors, teachers, and so on and so forth. The nearest you're going to get to a woman in the New Testament having any kind of role, if you will, will be Romans 16 where we meet Phebe, and she's called a servant of the church.

Now, in some of the new Bibles, that word **"servant"** is changed to **"deacon,"** which isn't any good, because deacon, according to 1 Timothy, is a man with a wife and children, and the early church didn't have any female pastors or deacons or elders or bishops. That's all come much later. In fact, it's modern-day feminism which has introduced this into the modern church. If you go back pre World War II, you won't find any women in any of the main denominations in any position of authority. Even though women make up the majority of members in any typical church, you won't find them in any position of authority.

Another issue I want to just quickly cover before we move on, it's interesting the amount of attention that the Church of England gets when it comes to women becoming bishops. I believe that there will be bishops in the Church of England quite possibly before the end is out. They've already got their vicars in and the deacons and deaconesses and archdeacons and these lovely titles they give themselves, but we don't hear a lot of noise about some of the "discrimination" that the Catholic church put on their women. And we've said in previous videos that one of the biggest advocates for human rights, especially for women, is Cherie Blair, Mrs. Booth, and Cherie Blair, as far as I know, hasn't taken her church to court over discrimination, and you would have thought if there were a handful of women in the Catholic church – and there are a handful of women in the Catholic church that would love to be priests – you would have thought that Ms. Booth or Ms. Blair – whatever title she uses – would take up their cause, and she hasn't done it. But nonetheless, the Lord Jesus Christ only chose apostles; He only chose men to take the Gospel out. And we've done other videos on that, so I shan't go over that again.

Okay. Back to Matthew 24. Going on from 24 and 25, you get the ten virgins, and I'll do another video on the ten virgins on another occasion. Just a couple of things to show you. Verse 11, the virgins are wanting the Lord to open the door to let them in, and verse 12 Jesus says, **"Verily I say unto you, I know you not."** Now, if you are born again, if you know the Lord, if you're bone of His bone and flesh of His flesh, He can't deny you. There's only one salvation in the Bible, and that is eternal salvation. And 2 Timothy 2:12 says if we suffer, we shall also reign with Him, and I believe that's a reference to the Millennium. If we deny Him, He will also deny us. Look at 13: **"If we believe not, yet he abideth faithful: he cannot deny himself."** If you started out with Christ and you were actually born again and one of His, then you will always be one of His. You can fall away into apostasy – and I'll just show you a reference for that – and if you fall away altogether and become an unbeliever, then according to 1 John 2:19, you were never of the Lord's. And it says, **"They went out from us, but they were not of us; for if they had been of us, they would no doubt have continued with us: but they went out, that they might be made manifest that they were not all of us."** In other words, these people that went out from the early church were never true believers in the first place. And that's the issue, isn't it? It's not that you were once saved and you lost your salvation. No. You were never saved to begin with.

And Matthew 7:21 and 22 is going to be a cross reference to Matthew 25, and it says, **"Not every one that saith unto me, Lord, Lord, shall enter into the kingdom of heaven; but he that doeth the will of my Father which is in heaven."** Now, what is the will of the Father? Well, John 6 says it's to believe on Jesus as the Messiah, to believe on Him as the Saviour of the world. There's no works involved; it's simply to believe on Him – total belief. 22: **"Many will say to me in that day"** – this is really, I think, a reference to the Great White Throne, but we can use this spiritually, anyway, in reference to this video – **"Lord, Lord"** – again, they call Him Lord twice; these aren't atheists; these are religious people – **"Lord, Lord, have we not prophesied in thy name?"** – these are people that think the gifts are still for today – **"and in thy name have cast out devils?"** – again, these are your modern-day exorcists – **"and in thy name done many wonderful works?"** – these people think that their works are going to save them – **"And then will I profess unto them, I never knew you: depart from me, ye that work iniquity."** Again, here is a clear picture of a group of people that were never saved, and He says, **"I never knew you. Depart from me."** So I don't believe that once saved you can be lost. That's, really, conditional security, and I've done so many videos on eternal security that I won't go over those all again.

But I just thought it would be worth just covering a few verses before we move on to the Rapture, *harpazo*, which we've also spoken about in previous videos, and then we'll look at the man of sin. And like I said at the beginning of part 1, I don't know how long these videos are going to last, and hopefully you're finding these of some interest, and if not, let me know. But as always, we look forward to hearing from you, and we'll continue to push on as the Lord leads.

Okay. We finished last time going through Matthew 24, and we looked at pre-millennialism, a-mill, and post-mill. And I think it's fair to say since the fourth century, a man called Augustine – probably the first real Roman Catholic – decided that the idea of a thousand year reign was farcical, and he took on the position of a-millennial, which was later picked up by a lot of the Reformers, and probably just after the Second Vatican Council, post-millennialism became very popular as well. But I think in reality the two have run pretty much side-by-side since the fourth century. A lot of the early church leaders were pre-millennial, and John Calvin said that the idea of a millennial reign was "childish."

Okay. Now, when we go through the Scripture, one thing you will see is that sometimes just a comma will separate two dispensations. For example, if you go to Acts Chapter 2 verse 16: **"But this is that which was spoken by the prophet Joel"** – and it quotes now from Joel – **"And it shall come to pass in the last days, saith God, I will pour out my Spirit upon all flesh: and your sons and your daughters shall prophesy, and your young men shall see visions, and your old men shall dream dreams."** Again, that's from the book of Joel, third chapter, I believe. And Joel is a Jewish writer, again, writing to the Jews, and Acts Chapter 2 is picked up by Dr. Luke – another Jew – who's also writing to the Jews. It said **"your sons and your daughters will prophesy,"** and there are different areas of prophecy. There's telling the future, which is one form of a prophecy like Simeon, and then there's prophesying as in giving God the glory and the praise like Philip's daughters. There's a distinction there, of course. Eighteen, **"And on my servants and on my handmaidens I will pour out in those days of my Spirit: and they shall prophesy."**

Now, look at this, verse 19. Just a colon separates two dispensations. Now, as I say, verses 16, 17, and 18 are fulfilled from the time of Christ, if you think of Simeon and Anna, up till the day of Pentecost and beyond; but by verse 19, **"And I will show wonders in heaven above,"** didn't happen at Pentecost **"and signs in the earth beneath; blood, and fire, and vapor of smoke"** – again, it didn't happen at the First Advent.

Twenty: **"The sun shall be turned into darkness, and the moon into blood, before that great and notable day of the Lord come."** Again, it didn't happen at the First Advent. So there you see from verses 18 to 19 there's two dispensations, and just a colon separates it. And 21: **"And it shall come to pass, that whosoever shall call on the name of the Lord shall be saved,"** and that is a reference to Isaiah initially, and in Isaiah it's referring to Jehovah God, and here Luke quotes it and puts it to Jesus Christ, and that's why we believe that Jesus is God.

Just another quick footnote on the area of the deity of Christ. I never ever get tired of trying to show people the deity of Christ – Acts 20, I think it is, Acts 20 verse 28: **"Take heed therefore unto yourselves, and to all the flock, over the which the Holy Ghost hath made you overseers, to feed the church of God, which he hath purchased with his own blood."** Okay. So God has purchased the church with His own blood. If you go to Colossians 1:20, **"And, having made peace through the blood of his cross, by him to reconcile all things unto himself"** – again, a reference to Christ. Jesus Christ is God. Acts 20 speaks about the blood of God, and in Colossians Chapter 1 verse 20 you see it's referring to the Son of God.

First Thessalonians Chapter 1 verse 9: **"For they themselves show of us what manner of entering in we had unto you, and how ye turned to God from idols to serve the living and true God."** Look at verse 10 – **"And to wait for his Son from heaven, whom he raised from the dead, even Jesus, which delivered us from the wrath to come."** That is a reference to the Rapture. We are to wait for Jesus to come for us. And if you go to Mark 14, I think it is, Mark 14 – it's the last verse – make it 13, Mark 13:37, last verse, Mark 13:37: **"And what I say unto you I say unto all, Watch."** Now, you were told to watch for the Son of man. Now, you weren't told to watch for the Antichrist, and you weren't told to watch for the false prophet, and you weren't told to store up food and other necessities for the Great Tribulation. You were told to wait for the Son who's going to come from Heaven.

Back to Acts Chapter 1, the book of Acts, I should say, Acts Chapter 1 verse 9: **"And when he had spoken these things, while they beheld, he was taken up; and a cloud received him out of their sight. And while they looked steadfastly towards heaven as he went up, behold, two men stood by them in white apparel; Which also said, Ye men of Galilee, why stand ye gazing up into heaven? this same Jesus, which is taken up from you into heaven, shall so come in like manner as you have seen him go into heaven."** Only the church saw Christ go up into glory, and only the church is going to see Him come back at the Rapture.

First Thessalonians Chapter 3:13: **"To the end he may establish your hearts unblamable in holiness before God, even our Father, at the coming of our Lord Jesus Christ with all his saints."** That is a reference to the Second Advent when Christ comes back to the earth, Matthew 24, not of the Rapture. The Rapture He comes on His own and He catches up to meet Him in space. Chapter 4:14: **"For if we believe that Jesus died and rose again"** – no works involved there – **"even so them also which sleep in Jesus will God bring back with him."** Those that have slept will obviously go up in the Rapture, which we get from the next verse: **"For this we say unto you by the word of the Lord, that we which are alive and remain unto the coming of the Lord shall not prevent them which are asleep"**; **"For the Lord** himself shall descend from heaven with a shout, with the voice of the archangel, and with the trump of God: and the dead in Christ shall rise first.**" And here you have some kind of angelic proclamation that He's coming for His church. And verse 17: **"And then we which are alive and remain shall be caught up together with them in the clouds to meet the Lord in the air, and so shall we ever be with the Lord, wherefore comfort one another with these words."** No mention of the Tribulation here, just the Rapture, and that's one of the reasons why we're told to be holy and always be on the watch, on the lookout for the Lord's return. We don't want to be caught in sin or living an immoral life. We want to be clean and holy to the best of our ability.

Now Chapter 5 verse 1: **"But of the times and the seasons, brethren, ye have no need that I write unto you. For yourselves know perfectly that the day of the Lord so cometh as a thief in the night. For when they shall say, Peace and safety; then sudden destruction cometh upon them, as travail upon a woman with child; and they shall not escape. But ye, brethren, are not in darkness, that that day should overtake you as a thief."**

Again, you've got two parts of the Second Advent here, and just a couple of verses distinguish the Rapture from the Second Advent when He comes back to the earth and takes vengeance according to 2 Thessalonians 1:7: **"And to you who are troubled rest with us, when the Lord Jesus shall be revealed from heaven with His mighty angels, In flaming fire taking vengeance on them that know not God, and that obey not the gospel of our Lord Jesus Christ: Who shall be punished with everlasting destruction from the presence of the Lord, and from the glory of his power."**

That is the Second Advent when He comes back to the earth, and you can cross reference that with Revelation 19:14: **"And the armies which were in heaven followed him upon white horses, clothed in fine linen, white and clean."** So there was a distinction, as I've said in other videos, between the Rapture and the Second Coming when He comes to the earth to reign 1000 years.

Revelation 13:8: **"And all that dwell upon the earth shall worship him"** – there's your Antichrist – **"whose names are not written in the book of life of the Lamb slain from the foundation of the world."** That, of course, is a Tribulation passage, and I'll come back to the Tribulation in a minute.

Second Thessalonians 2 verse 8: **"And then shall that Wicked be revealed, whom the Lord shall consume with the spirit of His mouth, and shall destroy with the brightness of his coming."** This is a reference to the Antichrist, of course, the man of sin. **"Even him, whose coming is after the working of Satan with all power and signs and lying wonders, And with all deceivableness of unrighteousness in them that perish"** – Why? – **"because they received not the love of the truth that they might be saved."** I just want to say something quickly. This is speaking primarily of the Great Tribulation, but like most parts of Scripture, you can apply it spiritually to a lot of the people today who are living in the church age who are dead in trespasses and sin in religious organisations worshipping false gods, and according to verse 11, **"for this cause God shall send them strong delusion, that they should believe a lie: That they all might be damned who believed not the truth, but had pleasure in unrighteousness."**

Just go to Ezekiel 14:9 to see that the Lord will allow man to do what man wants to do because man by nature is depraved –14:9: **"And if the prophet be deceived when he hath spoken a thing, I the LORD have deceived that prophet, and I will stretch out my hand upon him, and will destroy him from the midst of my people Israel."** When you have false religions teaching heresies and millions and millions of people are caught up in those false religions, and you've been witnessing to these people, you've been praying for these people, you've been fasting for these people, and nothing you say makes any difference, then, according to this, the Lord is behind it, and there comes a time when you may have to leave certain people and just come away from them. Personally, I will always pray for a person as long as I can and only a last resort would I want to write a person off, because we don't know how far a person has gone in his or her life if they're not walking with the Lord Jesus.

Back to 2 Thessalonians 2:1: **"Now, we beseech you, brethren, by the coming of our Lord Jesus Christ, and by our gathering together unto him."** Matthew 24:31 would be a good cross-reference to that. The angels are going to gather those that are on the earth at the end of the Tribulation and take them into the Millennium. And it could also be a reference to the Rapture as well, 1 Thessalonians 4:16, but let's read on: **"That ye be not soon shaken in mind, or be troubled, neither by spirit, nor by word, nor by letter as from us, as that the day of Christ is at hand. Let no man deceive you by any means: for that day shall not come, except there come a falling away first, and that man of sin be revealed, the son of perdition; Who opposeth and exalteth himself above all that is called God, or that is worshiped; so that he as God sitteth in the temple of God, showing himself that he is God."**

Now, a lot of people are going to get sucked up and call out from the hysteria which is going to be surrounding the Antichrist. But don't forget the false prophets – Revelation. We've got two references in Revelation. There's probably more but I'm just going to give you two: Revelation 13:1: **"And I stood upon the sand of the sea, and saw a beast rise up out of the sea, having seven heads and ten horns, and upon his horns ten crowns, and upon his heads the name of blasphemy. And the beast which I saw was like unto a leopard, and his feet were as the feet of a bear, and his mouth as the mouth of a lion: and the dragon"** – that's Satan, of course – **"gave him his power, and his seat, and great authority."** Now, that expression **"seat"** is used in many religions to denote the position of authority. The Catholic church speaks about the seat or the chair of Peter, and this beast that comes out of the sea is going to have a seat, and he has great authority. **"And I saw one of his heads as it was wounded to death; and his deadly wound was healed: and all the world wondered after the beast. And they worshiped the dragon"** – again, that's Satan – **"which gave power unto the beast: and they worshiped the beast, saying, Who is like unto the beast? who is able to make war with him?"** Now, this beast here that comes out of the sea I believe is a reference to the Antichrist, and, as you can see, man not only worships the devil, but they're going to worship the beast too.

But let's read on: **"And there was given unto him a mouth speaking great things and blasphemies; and power was given unto him to continue forty and two months"** – forty-two months, which, of course, is three and a half years. **"And he opened his mouth in blasphemy against God, to blaspheme his name, and his tabernacle, and them that dwell in heaven. And it was given unto him to make war with the saints"** – There's your Tribulation saints, not the church age. These are the people that are saved in the Tribulation – **"and to overcome them"** – They're going to be martyred – **"and power was given him over all kindreds, and tongues, and nations."** Just keep that Scripture in mind, and Matthew Chapter 3, John speaks about the Lord Jesus and the power that He has. As you know, nothing can happen on this earth if the Lord doesn't give it to man – actually, make it John, John Chapter 3, John Chapter 3:27: **"John answered and said, A man can receive nothing, except it be given from heaven."** Every good thing and even every bad thing comes from heaven. These guys, these dictators – Stalin, Hitler, Pol Pot – they can't do anything unless the Lord gives them the green light, and the reason these guys do what they do is because God is angry with the wicked, and He hates all workers of iniquity, and His wrath is very much in the world at this moment.

Revelation 13:8: **"And all that dwell upon the earth shall worship him, whose names are not written in the book of life of the**

Lamb slain from the foundation of the world." And we've already looked at that from 2 Thessalonians 2. **"If any man have an ear, let him hear."** Go over to verse 11: **"And I beheld another beast coming up out of the earth; and he had two horns like a lamb, and he spake as a dragon. And he exerciseth all the power of the first beast before him, and causeth the earth and them which dwell therein to worship the first beast, whose deadly wound was healed."** Here is your false prophet, and maybe in the next video I'll look at the false prophet in a bit more light. But here you have an unholy trinity. You have the devil, who's obviously the power behind the scenes; the Antichrist, who is the beast which comes out of the sea; and then, of course, you have the false prophet which comes from the earth. Now, I've long thought that the false prophet will come from the religious realm, and the biggest religion in the world today, although by numbers, it is Islam, but by power, it is Roman Catholicism. And when we get to Revelation 17, you may agree with me that it will be the church of Rome that we have in mind here.

One of the main points which gets put across by those of us that are pre-tribulational is from Revelation 4 verse 1. It says this: **"After this I looked, and behold, a door was opened in heaven"** – of course, Jesus in the Gospel of John says He is the door, which as you would understand to be an entrance to the Father. Paul says in 1 Timothy 2:5 there's only one God and one mediator, and the mediator is Jesus Christ, and we have access straight to Heaven through Christ Himself. Revelation 4:1 – **"and the first voice which I heard was as it were of a trumpet talking with me; which said, Come up hither, and I will show thee things which must be hereafter."** Okay. That's a reference, that's a kind of a rapture. Paul is on the Isle of Patmos, and he is caught up to be shown a load of visions, which, of course, will play out throughout the next 2,000 years plus.

Just to show you that this sort of language isn't unheard of, 2 Corinthians 12:2: **"I knew a man in Christ above fourteen years ago,** (whether in the body, I cannot tell; or whether out of the body, I cannot tell: God knoweth;) such a one caught up to the third heaven." That, of course, is the apostle Paul speaking about himself and, again, a very clear picture of a rapture. But when you read through Revelation 4, you'll see that there are no mentions of the churches. It starts in Chapter 2. You've got the church of Ephesus, Smyrna, Pergamos, Thyatira, Sardis, Philadelphia, and Laodicea – seven churches – but by Chapter 4, the churches have gone. And like I've said before, the whole area of the Great Tribulation is in reference to Israel; and, of course, if you go to Revelation 11, you'll see that the Lord is going to do something quite amazing. Romans 11 verse 1: **"Hath God cast away his people? God forbid."** Go down to 11: **"Have they stumbled that they should fall? God forbid"**; 15, **"For if the casting away of them be the reconciling of the world, what shall the receiving of them be, but life from the dead? For if the first fruit be holy"** – verse 16 – **"the lump is also holy: and if the root be holy, so are the branches"**; 20, **"Well; because of unbelief they were broken off, and thou standest by faith. Be not highminded, but fear: For if God spared not the natural branches, take heed lest he also spare not thee"**; 23, **"And they also, if they abide not still in unbelief, shall be grafted in: for God is able to graft them in again"**; 25, **"For I would not, brethren, that ye should be ignorant of this mystery, lest ye should be wise in your own conceits; that blindness in part is happened to Israel, until the fulness of the Gentiles be come in. And so all Israel shall be saved: as it is written, There shall come out of Sion the Deliverer, and shall turn away ungodliness from Jacob"**; 29, **"For the gifts and calling of God are without repentance"**; 32, **"For God hath concluded them all in unbelief, that he might have mercy upon all."**

Zechariah 12 verse 10: **"And I will pour upon the house of David, and upon the inhabitants of Jerusalem, the spirit of grace and of supplications:"** – and look at this – **"and they shall look upon me whom they have pierced, and they shall mourn for him, as one mourneth for his only son, and shall be in bitterness for him, as one that is in bitterness for his firstborn." Now, look at verse 9: "And it shall come to pass in that day, that I will seek to destroy all the nations that come against Jerusalem."

Now 14:3: "Then shall the LORD go forth, and fight against those nations, as when he fought in the day of battle. And his feet shall stand in that day upon the Mount of Olives, which is before Jerusalem on the east." Again, that's the Second Advent, not the Rapture.

13:7: "Awake, O sword, against my shepherd, and against the man that is my fellow, saith the LORD of hosts: smite the shepherd, and the sheep shall be scattered: and I will turn mine hand upon the little ones." Psalm 23 says, "The Lord is my shepherd," and the Gospel of John says that Christ is the good shepherd. And the Second Coming, verse 8, 13:8: "And it shall come to pass, that in all the land, saith the LORD, two parts therein shall be cut off and die; but the third shall be left therein." And there's your remnant of the Jews. A third are going to be saved. At the moment, you've got about 6 1/2 million Jews in Israel. So a third of 6 million is 2 million Jews. So only a third are going to be saved.

Zechariah 14:5: "And ye shall flee to the valley of the mountains; for the valley of the mountains shall reach unto Azal: yea, ye shall flee, like as ye fled from before the earthquake in the days of Uzziah king of Judah" – now watch this – "and the LORD my God shall come, and all the saints with thee." Again, Christ is called the Lord my God as He was by Thomas in John Chapter 20:28, I think it was. And here again "the Lord my God" is referring to Christ with His saints coming at the end of the Tribulation. How can that be? Well, they've been with Him throughout the Tribulation.

Zechariah Chapter 14:6: "And it shall come to pass in that day, that the light shall not be clear, nor dark." Matthew 24 again speaks about the darkness, stars falling from heaven, and also you might want to take a look at Joshua. I won't read it. I haven't got time. But Joshua – I think it's Joshua 10. I'll give you correct Scripture for it. Joshua 10:12-13. And back to Zechariah 14:9: **"And the LORD shall be king over all the earth: in that day shall there be one LORD, and his name one."** That, of course, is a reference to the thousand-year reign, and I may return to that once again in the next video.

REVELATION 1

Okay. This series of clips will be primarily focusing on the book of Revelation. Just a few things to say before I get into this multiple batch of clips. First of all, Revelation normally takes about three hours for me to read it, and I read pretty quickly. But when I go through the Scripture, I deliberately read rather slowly. There is so much material in Revelation that three hours is probably a conservative amount of time that it takes me to read it properly and get a lot of information from it. I'll just give you an example. I've read 11 chapters. I'm up to Chapter 12, and I've just stopped at the end of Chapter 11, and I've already accumulated three A4 sheets of paper, thoughts and comments, as I've gone through it, and I'm going to share those with you now.

Also, I just want to say that when you read the book of Revelation, a lot of people don't like this book, and it's one of the reasons why so few churches will even look at it. Luther put the book of James after Revelation because he didn't like James due to his position on works and faith and justification before man and justification before God. And Revelation was also a neglected book by most of the Reformers too, I should say. Calvin was the worst of the Reformers when it came to his understanding of Bible prophecy. But I just want to say that when you read Revelation, you need to be mindful that the subject and the theological term of literalism comes into play, and literalism simply means that if you're not careful, you take every verse, not only in Revelation but in the whole Bible, to be a literal rendering.

Now, I'm a literalist when I read the Scriptures. I don't spiritualise the Bible and the passages unless it's absolutely essential. Now, one of the cardinal rules of hermeneutics is you don't spiritualise a passage unless you have to, and if you've got five verses which are very clear on one area and one or two verses which seem to go against the majority, then the majority outweighs the minority. As with literalism, just keep it in mind that there are parts of Scripture, for example, in John 6, the eating and drinking of the Lord's body, and the Catholics take it literally, which is a mistake. And the Mormons also fall into literalism. And the Scriptures in the Old Testament that speak about the Lord as a bird and He covers His children with His feathers, and God isn't a bird. These same people that take the Scriptures literally don't take Matthew 5 literally when the Lord says to pluck your eye out and cut your hand off if you're doing things which you shouldn't be doing.

So just want to keep those things in mind when we go through Revelation today. Like I say, I take all of these Scriptures literally unless it's absolutely impossible, but even though Revelation is a very symbolic, very mystical book, there's just so much in here which we need to approach with reverence, and we ask the Lord to bless this in Jesus' name. Amen.

VERSE 1: **"The Revelation of Jesus Christ, which God gave unto him, to show unto his servants things which must shortly come to pass."**

And that expression **"shortly come to pass"** in today's understanding you would think it would be with an imminence, something which is going to occur like straightaway, but by verse 3 it says, **"these things that are written, for the time is at hand."** So keep those things that are written at hand. And in Matthew Chapter 3 Jesus says the Kingdom of Heaven is at hand.

VERSE 7, it says everybody will see Him. Now, when Christ comes back, all nations, all kindreds are going to see Him, and they're going to wail because of Him – a bit like Job. He wailed; and, of course, Job was a type of Israel during the Tribulation, a lot of suffering and pain, which we'll look at from Chapter 12 onwards. Like I said, the Rapture is only going to be witnessed by the church, those that are born again, whereas the Scripture Revelation 1:7, which I've just given you, is going to be witnessed by the whole world. It's a bit like Matthew Chapter 2 when the wise men went into Jerusalem and they went around all of Jerusalem asking everybody where the Son of God was born, and that was done deliberately, of course, so that the whole world, especially in Jerusalem, for that matter, would know that the Messiah had been born.

The first part of Revelation from Chapter 1 to 4 is for the seven churches in Asia, and by the end of Chapter 3 verse 22, it closes its message to the churches – very important to rightly divide the word of truth.

CHAPTER 2

VERSE 13 we find Satan's seat. Satan has a HQ, it would appear, and that is where he dwells, and the Lord says, **"I know thy works, and where thou dwellest, even where Satan's seat is: and thou holdest fast my name, and hast not denied my faith."** So even there in the hotbed of Satan's den the church has stood firm – a bit like Matthew 16, the gates of hell would not prevail against the church. We've had Communism; we've had fascism; we've had Romanism, evolution, every "ism" and every sect and every system – Freemasonry, Illuminati – all these groups have come, and the church, the true church, the church of the born again saint still stands as Matthew 16 said it would too.

VERSE 20 we find Jezebel, this woman Jezebel. Of course, we think of Jezebel and Ahab from the Old Testament, but here we find another Jezebel in the New Testament, and she has seduced the Lord's servants, and they are committing fornication. It could be spiritual fornication, and it could also be a physical fornication. But nonetheless, they are eating sacrifices unto idols, and that could be a form of reference to the Mass, the Roman Catholic Mass. They are very good at their non-bloody sacrifice, as they call it.

VERSE 21 says that the Lord has given her space to repent of her fornication, and she repented not. Therefore, He will **"cast her into a bed, and them which commit adultery with her into great tribulation, except they repent of their deeds"** (v. 22.) Once again, the Lord is always gracious, gives people time and time and time to repent, but, of course, men love darkness rather than light, and they won't repent simply because their sins are evident and they love their wickedness.

VERSE 23, and the Lord says He will **"kill her children with death; and all the churches shall know that I am he which searcheth the reins and hearts: and I will give unto every one of you according to your works."** So even the church isn't going to escape the chastisement of the Lord.

VERSES 26 and 27 speak about these that overcome and keep my works unto the end He will give power over the nations and rule them with a rod of iron. That, as far as I can see, is a reference to the thousand-year reign which Paul speaks about in 1 Corinthians 6 where he says we will judge angels.

CHAPTER 3

VERSE 9 is a reference to the synagogue of Satan which say they are Jews and are not, and the Lord says that He will make them to bow down at the feet of the church and know that He has loved us.

VERSE 10: **"Because thou hast kept the word of my patience, I also will keep thee from the hour of temptation, which will come upon all the world, to try them which dwell on the earth."**

Some people take that to be a reference to the Rapture, a calling out, and because those that have been faithful won't go through the Tribulation. Now, as far as I know, not many people are faithful and worthy to escape anything, even the saved people. So I'm not completely convinced that Chapter 3:10 is a clear, unequivocal reference to the Rapture. But I'm happy to stand corrected on that if necessary.

And, like I said, Chapter 3:22: **"He that hath an ear, let him hear what the Spirit saith unto the churches."**

So chapters 1 to 3 conclude with a closure to the churches.

CHAPTER 4

VERSE 1, John is taken up to Heaven – again, a picture of the church and the Tribulation – and he's shown things which will shortly, once again, come to pass.

CHAPTER 5

VERSE 10 of Chapter 5, only the redeemed reign on the earth, which would be pretty common sense, really. Only those that are saved are going to reign with Jesus for a thousand years.

CHAPTER 6 VERSE 2, the white horse has a bow but no arrow, and he has a crown. Now, some people think this to be the Lord Jesus Christ. I don't. I think this is the Antichrist. Of course, the Antichrist is a carbon copy, he's a counterfeit of the true Christ, and he comes to earth. And there's no mention of what he actually does, only that he conquers those on the earth but nothing about death because, of course, he is going to deceive people. He won't do it himself – a bit like Hitler and Stalin. Hitler and Stalin never killed anybody themselves, but they gave the order to their lieutenants to go out and do the killing – and probably what the Antichrist will do.

VERSE 4, another horse. This one is a red horse. He has power, and he can take the peace, and others will kill one another. So he's going to really upset the apple cart, and murders are going to occur due to the second of the horsemen.

VERSE 5 is a black horseman, and he has a pair of balances in his hand. So this third horseman is quite possibly going to be playing games with those on the earth. But he can't kill the oil and the wine, and that's quite probably a reference to the redeemed.

VERSE 8, the pale horse. He has power to kill a quarter of the earth. Now, what you will notice is a lot of these killings are going to be overlapping by the time we get to the end of Chapter 11.

VERSE 12, earthquake and darkness are upon the earth. And, again, darkness in the Bible, as you know, is always a picture of judgment, and Matthew 24 and Joshua 10 speak of the darkness and the moon becoming as blood.

VERSE 13, the stars fall from heaven. Stars in the Bible normally are a reference to angels.

VERSE 14, all the mountains and islands move out of their place. Now, I am a futurist – I think most of you know that now – and my question is this: When have these events happened? Have they already happened? I don't think they have happened. These are still future events; I'm convinced of it.

VERSES 15 and 17, the kings of the earth know that God is behind all of this. Judgment has come to them, and they even say the great day has come, and they call on the rocks to fall on them; but, of course, they won't repent because man is in rebellion to the Lord.

CHAPTER 7

VERSE 1, the angels stop the wind blowing on the earth. Of course, without the wind, without the air, we all die. We all need air. Some people take this expression **"standing on the four corners of the earth"** to somehow suggest that the Bible is backward. But we have North, East, West, and South. We have four parts of the globe. And it wasn't long ago when you had the expression "the British Empire stands on the four corners of the earth" – just a bit of figurative language. And we know from the Old Testament that the earth was round many years before it was discovered to be round. So we don't want to fall into that ignorance which has been put forward by people in the past that the earth is flat and Revelation 7 suggests that. No. It's just a figure of speech, as I say.

VERSE 3, the 144,000 are sealed in their foreheads with the seal of God, and these 144,000, according to verse 4, are the tribes of Israel – all of the tribes of Israel, not just some – all of the 12 tribes. Of course, Dan is omitted from here due to his apostasy.

VERSE 9, scores are saved, no doubt through these 144,000 witnessing, and they are straight in the glory of God. They go to Heaven directly – no purgatory, no sleeping in the ground like the Old Testament saints did prior to the Lord's death, burial, and resurrection.

These saved people go straight to be with the Lord Jesus Christ, and, of course, they are the Tribulation saints, not the church-age saints.

CHAPTER 8

VERSES 3-5 are also pretty daunting in some ways. You have the prayers of the saved which are in Heaven calling for judgment on those on the earth – fire and brimstone from Heaven. Like I said in the previous video or a couple of videos ago, when Stephen was put to death, he doesn't call for any judgment, but when Jeremiah was being severely persecuted, he calls for judgment on his enemies. And here you have the souls of those that are in Heaven, which you can also find in Chapter 6, calling for vengeance, and the Lord grants their request. And, of course, a third of the trees get destroyed as well. Of course, no trees, there's nothing to breathe; there's no oxygen. You can see how this is working out. No doubt a lot of these events are overlapping. But this is a horrific period of judgment from the Lord, and I ask the question again: Has this occurred yet? I say no, absolutely not.

VERSE 8, a third part of the sea becomes like blood. Again, Moses is an Old Testament saint who turned the Egyptian river into blood when he was dealing with Pharaoh, another Old Testament type of Antichrist.

VERSE 9, death follows, and even the ships are destroyed. Now, the ships being destroyed is interesting because we go to Zechariah and it speaks about people's eyes falling out, and some commentators believe that nuclear weapons will be involved in the Tribulation and man is going to be forced to go back to a boat, ships, and so on and so forth. It's also worth noting that when British and American troops first went into Afghanistan nine years ago now, they were using horseback. Britain was using the household cavalry to get around the mountains. Their smart weapons didn't actually work, and when they went into the caves of Tora Bora, they weren't fighting with guns; they were fighting with knives, hand-to-hand combat.

VERSES 10-11, the third angel sounds, and a great star from heaven, burning as it were a lamp, falls upon a third part of the rivers and the fountains of waters; and, of course, these waters become bitter – poison, no doubt – and many men die.

VERSE 12 is an interesting Scripture. The sun and the moon are deliberately interfered with by an angel of the Lord, not _the_ Angel of the Lord, of course, but _an_ angel of the Lord, and that's going to have massive repercussions because if you mess about with the moon, it, as you know, is tied in with the oceans of the world and gravity and everything, so quite possibly tidal waves will occur. And, again, interfering with the sun is going to cause darkness. Not much fun being in the dark all the time – a picture of Hell.

VERSE 13, another angel was flying through the midst of Heaven rebuking those that are on the earth. So wherever man is, he cannot escape the judgment which the Lord is putting on the world.

CHAPTER 9

VERSE 1, a fifth angel has a key to the bottomless pit.

VERSE 3, these locusts are released to kill those that are without the seal – again, the non-elect.

VERSE 6, suicide will not be allowed by God. There will be no escape; there will be no cutting your wrists or taking tablets. The Lord will not allow people to commit suicide.

VERSE 11, the king of scorpions is called Abaddon – Abaddon in Hebrew, Apollyon in Greek. Now, the Jehovah's Witnesses have made a huge blunder here. Their literature suggests that Abaddon is Jesus Christ. What a blasphemy.

VERSE 14, loose the four angels bound in the river Euphrates, which, of course, is in Iraq. By 9:15, a third are going to be killed.

VERSE 16, two hundred thousand thousand of the three horsemen are also going to be used. Now, most commentaries I think suggest that this is something like 200 million. There's no word for million in Greek, so thousand is the highest numerical wording or lettering which is used by the translators in the King James to suggest a huge amount of people. And these are probably a demonic army. Some have also suggested that it could be something to do with the Chinese, but even they haven't got 200 million soldiers.

VERSE 18, these three horsemen kill a third. And, again, a lot of overlapping here of all the deaths that have occurred on the world scene.

CHAPTER 11

VERSES 1-2, John is told to measure the third Temple, the Tribulation Temple. And the courtyard is for the Gentiles, and they get it for three and a half years.

VERSE 3, the two witnesses are sent to prophesy for three and a half years. I just want to read that, because there's been a lot of talk about who these two witnesses are. 11:3, they're clothed in sackcloth and ashes; 6, and they **"have power to shut Heaven, that it rain not in the days of their prophecy"** – it could be Elijah – and they **"have power over waters to turn to blood, and to smite the earth with all plagues, as often as they will."** It could be Moses. Some have suggested it could be Enoch for Elijah because Enoch never died. But Enoch didn't appear at the Transfiguration and Elijah did. Elijah was taken in the Rapture – again, a picture of the church – whereas Moses was put to death, dies – a picture of Israel. So the jury is out as to who these two witnesses are, but as we read on, the beast from the bottomless pit kills them, verse 7.

Now, just before I close this batch of clips, I just want to look at these verses, because if you can remember some of the commentaries that you may have read say 2- or 300 years ago by non-futurists, non-dispensationalists, their views on all this would be from a historical perspective. And people like Spurgeon was a historicist when it came to the Scripture, and they believed that the parts of Revelation were being fulfilled throughout the church age, if you will. But I believe this is probably one of the strongest bits of Scripture for futurism.

And I just want to say something else just before I close. The Jesuits, as clever and as devious and as conniving as they are, shouldn't be given credit for everything that goes on in the world today. They didn't write the Bible. They may have forged books and publications and they may have infiltrated most of the Protestant denominations and they may be behind some of the worst terrorist attacks the world has seen, but the actual Scripture itself, especially the New Testament, there's no evidence that they've ever interfered with any of the New Testament Scriptures. Again, I'm reading a King James Bible here. This is the only true Protestant book. All the other Bibles consist from Catholic manuscripts, so the NIV, the New King James, the New Jerusalem Bible, yes, they are all Catholic bibles and certainly have got Jesuits' influence, but the King James Bible doesn't have any Jesuit or Catholic influence. So I'm not going to give the Jesuits all of the credit for a lot of the things that we see and hear in the world today. They're not that smart.

VERSES 8-9: "And their dead bodies shall lie in the street of the great city, which spiritually is called Sodom and Egypt, where also our Lord was crucified." This is Jerusalem, but here it's spiritually called Sodom and Egypt due to its wickedness; And they of the people and kindreds and tongues and nations shall see their dead bodies three days and a half, and shall not suffer their dead bodies to be put in graves."

Now, verse 9 suggests that the world is seeing what is going on here. Satellite television, computers, no doubt, is quite probable, and it's also fair to say that you could have a group of people that are in Jerusalem at that time who are made up of different nations. That's also possible. But look at verse 10:

VERSE 10: "And they that dwell upon the earth shall rejoice over them, and make merry, and shall send gifts one to another; because these two prophets tormented them that dwelt on the earth."

And how do these people know what's going on without modern communication?

VERSES 11-12: "And after three days and a half the Spirit of life from God entered into them, and they stood upon their feet; and great fear fell upon them which saw them. And they heard a great voice from heaven saying unto them, Come up hither. And they ascended up to heaven in a cloud; and their enemies beheld them."

If this isn't a reference to modern communications witnessing future events, then I don't know what else it is. As far as I'm concerned, this is probably the clearest argument that these are still future events, and if they're not future events, then who are these two witnesses? Would it be Calvin and Luther? Wesley and Spurgeon? I mean, who are these two witnesses here? If you're not a futurist and you're a historicist, who are they? These are two literal people.

You can't spiritualise verse 3; you can't use literalism on verse 3. These are two witnesses. Once they die, verse 13, there's a great earthquake, **"and the tenth part of the city fell, and in the earthquake were slain of men seven thousand: and the remnant were affrighted, and gave glory to the God of heaven."**

So, once again, the righteous are saved, taken up to glory, and judgment falls as a result of it. Scripture says that the Lord mourns the death of His saints.

By Verse 15, the world systems and kingdoms now belong to the Lord and His Christ, and by Verse 19, the Ark of the Covenant is spotted in Heaven. We know that Mussolini and Hitler spent a lot of money and a lot of time digging up the earth and going through parts of the world trying to find the Ark of the Covenant, and some people think it's in Ethiopia, but according to Chapter 11 verse 19 it is in Heaven.

CHAPTER 12

VERSES 1-2: "And there appeared a great wonder in heaven; a woman clothed with the sun, and the moon under her feet, and upon her head a crown of twelve stars: And she being with child cried, travailing in birth, and pained to be delivered."

I just want to stop there for a moment and just add a few thoughts. First of all, this is a sign in Heaven, not on earth. A lot of people have read this and have come to the conclusion this is happening on earth, when the Bible says it's happening in Heaven. And I'll come back to that in a minute.

Second, this is a reference to the nation of Israel. Some people read this and think it's a reference to Mary and never progress beyond that. This vision of Israel, she has 12 stars, and in the Bible, stars nearly always refer to angels, and I'll come back to that in a minute.

VERSE 2: "And she being with child cried, travailing in birth, and pained to be delivered."

This could be a reference to Eve, Genesis Chapter 2. The Lord said that women would be suffering in childbirth as a result of the fall, and here the nation of Israel is bringing forth a child, and indirectly Mary, of course, as a daughter of Israel is possibly in mind here as well. But as I say, the main theme is the nation of Israel, the apple of God's eye.

VERSE 3: "And there appeared another wonder in heaven; and behold a great red dragon, having seven heads and ten horns, and seven crowns upon his heads."

Heads, plural. China and Wales are the only two countries that I can think of that have the symbol of the dragon on their flag, and the Bible says that the dragon is the devil. Read on.

VERSE 4: "And his tail drew the third part of the stars of heaven, and did cast them to the earth: and the dragon stood before the woman which was ready to be delivered, for to devour her child as soon as it was born."

If you go back to the Gospel accounts, you see the wise men under the orders of Herod the Great desperately out to kill the Christ child.

And throughout the Bible you're always going to find people trying to overthrow the will of God. And in recent years the Third Reich has been the biggest block of Jew killers that we've known in recent years. And Herod is just one of many, many antichrists – or types of antichrists, I should say.

This idea of stars falling, if you go to Luke 10:18: **"I beheld Satan as lightning fall from heaven."** Look at 20. Scripture says, **"rejoice, because your names are written in heaven."** Here you have the apostles pre-Pentecost, and they've already been saved, and their salvation was dependent on their faith in the Lord.

I just want to squeeze something else in quickly. I think it's John 15 – make it 13, John 13:10: **"He that is washed needeth not, save to wash his feet, but is clean every whit: and ye are clean, but not all."** Again, here's a picture of saved men pre-Pentecost, and they were saved simply by believing on the Lord. And here you find water being used figuratively cleaning your feet, and it makes you physically clean. But the washing here that is spoken about is a spiritual washing which comes from the new birth, not from a H2O baptism.

And I'll just squeeze another one in quickly because I think you can never tire of dealing with a fact. And I was talking to a guy just today who was a Pentecostal, and he was giving out tracts where I normally give out tracts; and he is what you call a waterdog, as some of our Baptist friends call such people, and that expression means that he thinks that water saves him. But look at 1 Peter 3:20: **"Which sometime were disobedient, when once the longsuffering of God waited in the days of Noah, while the ark was a preparing, wherein few, that is, eight souls were saved by water."** Look at this: **"The like figure whereunto even baptism does also now save us (not the putting away of the filth of the flesh, but the answer of a good conscience toward God,) by the resurrection of Jesus Christ"** (v. 21.) You were told in Mark 16 that if you believed and were then baptized, you would be saved. Just a slight diversion out of Revelation back into how to be saved. Like I say, you can never get this straight, and we want people to be saved and to know that they are saved, not to think they're saved but to know they are saved according to 1 John 5:13.

Also, just go to John, John 12:31: **"Now is the judgment of this world: now shall the prince of this world be cast out."** Jesus comes. All the devils start kicking off, and there's a massive outpouring of exorcisms on the part of the apostles, and, of course the Lord Jesus Christ. Jesus dies, goes back to Heaven; the apostles go out and preach the Gospel, and by the end of Acts, that ministry seems to have ceased. If you go into the epistles, there's almost nothing mentioned about exorcisms or what to do with unclean spirits. If you go to Romans 16:20: **"And the God of peace shall bruise Satan under your feet shortly."** So, again, there was this time coming soon when he will be completely done away, but Hebrews 4 – just look at that quickly – and we haven't finished with Revelation yet. Hebrews 2:14: **"Forasmuch then as the children are partakers of flesh and blood, he also himself likewise took part of the same; that through death he might destroy him that had the power of death, that is, the devil."**

There's no doubt that the devil is severely wounded, and he's nowhere near as powerful as he used to be. Saying that, we don't want to underestimate his power. If you go to 2 Timothy 2:26, **"that they might recover themselves out of the snare of the devil, who are taken captive by him at his will,"** and Paul also speaks about handing people over to Satan for the destruction of the flesh, which is a reference to excommunication, putting people out of a fellowship due to their wilful sin.

Go to Isaiah 14, Isaiah 14:12: **"How art thou fallen from heaven, O Lucifer, son of the morning! how art thou cut down to the ground, which didst weaken the nations!"** That term "O Lucifer" – I believe it's Latin – means light-bearer, and I was reading only recently – I think somebody sent me an e-mail saying that the words Lucifer,

Satan, and the devil are not referring to the same person, which is absolute madness. They certainly are. Thirteen: **"For thou hast said in thine heart, I will ascend into heaven, I will exalt my throne above the stars of God"** – and stars, angels. **"I will sit also upon the mount of the congregation, in the sides of the north: I will ascend above the heights of the clouds. I will be like the most high."** So this devil here certainly had plans to be something special, and, of course, he is turned into a serpent in Genesis 3.

And Paul also speaks about the devil in 2 Corinthians, not only 4:4 where he's called the god of this world – and that is also used to explain some of the blindness which so many people are experiencing – but 2 Corinthians 11:13, 14, and 15 speak about the devil turning himself into an angel of light, and also his ministers are able to do likewise. So he's certainly still around; he hasn't retired.

But looking at Revelation, because this is a sign in Heaven which is dealing with the First and Second Advent. In fact, reading through Revelation 12, I'm not sure it's even in chronological order, but let's read on and see what else we see.

VERSE 5: "And she brought forth a man child, who was to rule all nations with a rod of iron: and her child was caught up unto God, and to his throne."

Now, that expression **"to rule all nations with a rod of iron"** is a reference to the Second Advent. Psalm 110 – let's just go there a minute. Psalm 110 talks about Christ's coming back. Psalm 110:6: **"He shall judge among the heathen, he shall fill the places with the dead bodies; he shall wound the heads over many countries. He shall drink of the brook in the way: therefore shall he lift up the head."** That, again, hasn't happened, but at the Second Advent it certainly will happen. The child is caught up unto God and to His throne. That would have to be a reference to the ascension, of course. So the first thing is, there is a sign in Heaven. The birth of Christ obviously took place on earth, and John has seen a sign in Heaven relaying an image of something happening in earth 4 BC. Again, this Bible is such an amazing book that you need to be so careful when you read it that you don't miss these things.

VERSE 6: "And the woman fled into the wilderness, where she hath a place prepared of God, that they should feed her there a thousand two hundred and threescore days."

Again, that's three and a half years. We know from the Gospel accounts that Jesus went into Egypt until Archelaus, Herod's son, was dead. But he wasn't there for three and a half years because Matthew 2 says that the young children, the sons of Israel that Herod was looking for were about 18 months or so. And we also know that when Jesus died on the cross, Mary went to live with John, along with her other children, and, of course, Jesus was the oldest and therefore He was responsible for His mother's welfare. But you can't read 6 and put that on Mary. Clearly this is a reference to the nation of Israel, and I think it has a greater significance in the Second Coming, which, of course, is still future.

VERSES 7-8: "And there was war in heaven: Michael and his angels fought against the dragon; and the dragon fought and his angels, And prevailed not; neither was their place found any more in heaven."

Now, this has always been a very interesting bit of Scripture because you would have thought when the devil fell back in the garden – of course, he fell long before that, according to Isaiah 14 – but when you have the written word that he fell with Adam and Eve sinning, you would have thought that he would never have come into contact with the Lord. Job Chapter 1 speaks about Satan walking in the earth and through the earth, but that is a period probably in the times of Abraham or maybe even before Abraham, so even then he had access into Heaven. But even here, whether this is the First Coming or Second Coming, it's still quite recent in human years. It's still recent in modern times that the devil still has access to the Lord.

VERSE 9: "And the great dragon was cast out, that old serpent, called the Devil, and Satan, which deceiveth the whole world: he was cast out into the earth, and his angels were cast out with him."

Again, they volunteered to go with him, which we know is a suicide mission because the Bible says how it's all going to end up, and that's one of the reasons why these angels cannot be redeemed. First John speaks about us being the sons of God, which, according to Job 1, is a reference to angels. So it looks like the church, the sons of God, which refer to women as well, are going to somehow replace the fallen angels.

VERSE 10: "And I heard a loud voice saying in heaven, Now is come salvation, and strength, and the kingdom of our God, and the power of his Christ: for the accuser of our brethren is cast down, which accused them before our God day and night."

The word **"devil"** and **"Satan"** means slanderer. Jesus says you are a liar and you are a liar from the beginning. He's the father of lies. In fact, just go to Matthew 4 – actually make it Luke 4. Luke 4 is the parallel passage to Matthew 4, and, yes, verse 3: **"And the devil said unto him, if Thou be the Son of God, command this stone that be made bread. And Jesus answered him, saying, It is written, That man shall not live by bread alone, but by every word of God."** Now look at 5: **"And the devil, taking him up into a high mountain, showed unto him all the kingdoms of the world in a moment of time. And the devil said unto him, All this power will I give thee, and the glory of them: for that is delivered unto me; and to whomsoever I will I give it."** Now, I've often wondered, the devil is called the liar; he's called the slanderer; he's a deceiver. He may think he has all this power, but it doesn't mean he does have all this power. He is called the god of this world, but that's used in a derogatory sense. We know that the ultimate power in this universe comes from the Godhead, from the Triune God. Satan is simply a created being. Yes, he's a cherub, which is a higher form of angel, but I'm not sure that verse 6 means what he would want you to think it means, if that makes any sense.

Seven, **"If thou therefore wilt worship me, all shall be thine. And Jesus answered and said unto him, Get thee behind me, Satan: for it is written, Thou shalt worship the Lord thy God, and him only shalt thou serve."** Now, here he is claiming deity – Christ. He calls Himself the Lord thy God, and, yes, He doesn't correct the devil, which is correct. Some people say, "Well, if the devil didn't have the authority, then Jesus would have corrected him." Well, not always. There are other occasions in the Bible when people make an incorrect statement in regards to what the Lord has told them, and He doesn't correct them; He leaves them as they are simply as a sign of judgment on them. So just a little thing to share with you. But I'm certainly not negating the fact that the devil is a powerful being who shouldn't be messed around with. But he certainly has been wounded, anyway, through the cross of Christ.

VERSE 11: **"And they overcame him by the blood of the Lamb, and by the word of their testimony; and they loved not their lives unto the death."**

Now, some people read that as if works are involved, and I've done a video on Lordship salvation, so I won't go over that again. But if you go to 1 John, I want to show you something, a cross reference to Revelation 12:11. First John 5:5: **"Who is he that overcometh the world, but he that believeth that Jesus is the Son of God?"** And if you're still not sure, go to John 6 – Scripture with Scripture, Sola Scriptura. John 6:29: **"This is the work of God, that you believe on him whom he hath sent."** I'll give you one more, 40: **"And this is the will of him that sent me, that every one which seeth the Son, and believeth on him, may have everlasting life: and I will raise him up at the last day."** You want to be saved simply by faith in the finished work of the Lord Jesus Christ.

VERSE 12: **"Therefore rejoice, ye heavens, and ye that dwell in them. Woe to the inhabiters of the earth and of the sea! for the devil**

is come down unto you, having great wrath, because he knoweth that he hath but a short time."

Now, again, **"short time"** in the Bible doesn't mean it's going to happen in the next few minutes. It can mean a period of thousands of years because time with the Lord means nothing. The Lord lives outside of time. But in the ultimate plan of eternity, it is a short period of time.

VERSE 13: "And when the dragon saw that he was cast unto the earth, he persecuted the woman which brought forth the man child."

And there's no doubt that Israel has been attacked time and time and time again, not only with Islam, Communism, Nazism, but also replacement theology. Like I said in a couple of videos gone by, Augustine was one of the first people to believe that the church replaced Israel, and he did that for many different reasons. I think one of the main reasons was because of power, and I've done another video which I'll cover that on another occasion. But unfortunately, Augustine was the father of that modern-day thought, and unfortunately the Reformers – a lot of them, anyway, if not most of them – regurgitated it, and most of the churches today are also into replacement theology. And, of course, it does squeeze Israel in the minds of Christians out of the will of God, and therefore a lot of Christian churches are siding with Islam and other left-wing organisations against the nation of Israel, something we need to be very, very careful that we don't do as pre-millennial Christians.

VERSE 14: "And to the woman were given two wings of a great eagle, that she might fly into the wilderness, into her place, where she is nourished for a time, and times, and half a time, from the face of the serpent."

Now, I've often thought of this expression **"two wings of a great eagle,"** and if you look at the American flag, it's not an eagle; they have a phoenix on their flag, and, of course, America is Israel's closest friend in a political sense, whereas the Christians are America's closest spiritual friend, and since '48, America's been very, very good to Israel. She's armed Israel; she's trained Israel. But in recent years there's been a lot of pressure put on Israel, especially with the peace talks. And the Peace Quartet and all these things won't come to anything because the Bible says there will never be peace until, of course, Christ comes back. And we'll look at Daniel on another video. But here you find a reference to this great eagle, and she takes Israel and looks after her, if you will.

VERSE 15: "And the serpent cast out of his mouth water as a flood after the woman, that he might cause her to be carried away of the flood."

Simply that, so no more than probably a local flood aimed at Israel. And the devil does have power over nature. That's nothing new there, of course.

VERSE 16: "And the earth helped the woman, and the earth opened her mouth, and swallowed up the flood which the dragon cast out of his mouth."

Two things to say here. First of all, the term **"earth"** can mean the literal ground under your feet, but like in the Old Testament when Moses took vengeance on the idolaters and the ground literally sucked them under, sucked them in, it could be a reference to the literal ground under your feet, but it could possibly be a reference to people. And we know in Matthew 25 the Lord will separate the sheep from the goats, and there are a lot of commentators who believe that in the Tribulation those that treat the Jew well are going to be rewarded, and that's possible. But either way, the world has helped in 16, and they've saved the woman. Now, look at 17:

VERSE 17: "And the dragon was wroth with the woman, and went to make war with the remnant of her seed, which keep the commandments of God, and have the testimony of Jesus Christ."

If that is a reference to the Virgin Mary, what is this speaking about? It talks about her seed. Her own literal seed? Her own children? No. It's talking to Israel. It's speaking about the nation of Israel, of course. These are Jewish Christians that keep the commandments of God and the testimony of Jesus Christ.

Just before I close this video, I just want to give you another cross-reference and then wrap this part on the 12th Chapter of Revelation up. There are some dispensationalists that believe that in the Tribulation, you need to have faith and works to be saved, and they quote Matthew 24: **"He that shall endure unto the end, the same shall be saved,"** which is found in Matthew 10 and Matthew 24, and that endurance, they believe, is what will give you everlasting life – you believe in the Lord, you endure, you keep the law, you keep the Sabbath and probably get circumcised, and it's a complete throwback to the Old Testament.

When we look at Romans 4, Paul says that Abraham, who was before the law, was saved by his faith in the Lord, and Paul says that's how Abraham got saved and that's how you're going to get saved. And I agree with that and I take it through to the Tribulation too, because if we go to the system which some of these guys hold to that in the Tribulation it's going to be faith and works, not only are you creating a two-tier system, you're also going to have a lot of boasting going on in eternity. You're going to have people saved in the Tribulation who did it their way – they got saved and they got circumcised and they did this and they did that – and then you have the church-age saints who simply believed on the Lord. And it's not too much of a stretch to think, "Is there going to be some kind of bickering going on?" I don't know. But I know one thing that if you're a Calvinist, you would argue that faith is a gift of God. Now, I believe that grace, according to Ephesians 2, is the gift of God, and, yes, Paul does speak about faith being one of the gifts in 1 Corinthians, but in that reference, it's a faith, as I understand it, to be like a missionary faith to do something very special for the Lord.

So I don't want to get into this trap that in the Tribulation it needs to be faith and works to get saved, because I think that's going to be impossible. No one is going to be good enough to keep the law. Nobody was able to keep it in the Old Testament, and even in Acts 15 the early church was complaining about how they couldn't keep the law either.

So what are these commandments which we find in Revelation 12? Okay. Go to 1 John 3:21: **"Beloved, if our heart condemn us not, then have we confidence toward God. And whatsoever we ask, we receive of him, because we keep his commandments, and do those things that are pleasing in his sight. And this is his commandment, That we should believe on the name of his Son Jesus Christ"** – that would be Acts 16, Romans 10, John 5:24 – **"and love one another, as he gave us commandment. And he that keepeth his commandments dwelleth in him, and he in him. And hereby we know that he abideth in us, by the Spirit which he hath given us."**

So you believe in the Lord Jesus Christ, which would be found throughout the New Testament, and you love your fellow believer.

CHAPTER 13

VERSE 1: "And I stood upon the sand of the sea, and saw a beast rise up out of the sea, having seven heads and ten horns, and upon his horns ten crowns, and upon his heads the name of blasphemy."

First of all, you will see that John is standing on the sand of the sea, and I would take that to be a reference that he's back on the earth, back on the Isle of Patmos. And at the end of Chapter 10, he was told to prophesy again before many peoples, nations, tongues, and kings; so even in his old age, his work isn't finished, and that should be a good plug to put out to those that are up in years to keep on going and those that are young in years to double your efforts. There's much work to be done if you're a Christian. Don't just think that you've done this or you've done that and therefore you don't need to do anymore. You were told to be ready in season and out of season; and there's always work to be done for the Lord, and if you want some ideas or tips, then drop us a line, and we'll be happy to share them with you.

This beast coming out of the sea, according to Isaiah 27 verse 1 – again, Scripture with Scripture – and it says: **"In that day the LORD with his sore and great and strong sword shall punish leviathan the piercing serpent, even leviathan that crooked serpent; and he shall slay the dragon that is in the sea."** Clearly the beast coming out of the sea, I would cross reference that to Isaiah and have it as being the dragon; and, of course, the dragon, according to verse 4 of Revelation 13, is Satan. The beast coming out of the sea isn't going to be human, although he'll have a human body and people will be able to see him and speak to him, but he will be supernatural. He's going to be controlled by the devil; he'll be the devil's incarnate man on the earth, and he'll be completely possessed by the devil. In reality, he will be Satan with a human body. A lot of people think that Judas Iscariot has a part to play in this, but I don't. That's not to say he doesn't play any part whatsoever in eschatology, but I don't have him coming up out of the sea.

I just want to add a footnote before I go on. Reformed Christians take the position that the office of the papacy is the Antichrist, but for that to fit with Revelation 13, they would have to then argue that the popes that we've had – and we've had about 260 plus if you go with the Catholic church's count, and I severely dispute that. There are many times when their popes weren't even counted. But let's say you add a couple of hundred, just for argument's sake, would they then be saying that all of these popes were not human, were demonic? I've never heard that. But they'd have to go down that road according to 13:1. I would say that the popes are false prophets, according to verse 11, and there's still a future for false prophets, and some Catholic mystics believe that the pope after this pope will be Peter II, and this Peter II they claim will be the last pope, an antipope. That's just a Catholic mysticism, but nonetheless, I thought it might be worth sharing it with you. I will say this, though, that the papacy is certainly the biggest type of antichrist in post-apostolic days – no doubt whatsoever about that – but to say that the popes themselves will be the man of sin is problematic, and I'll come back to that in a minute.

We've got to remember when reading this book, this is a Jewish book. The Jews are the people of the Lord. Paul says they may be enemies for our sake, but they are beloved for the Father's sake. And because we live in an age now where Gentiles pretty much dominate the so-called Christian world, Christendom, we've lost sight that this is a Jewish book. And the Jews are not going to take a Gentile as their long-awaited Messiah. Go to John 5:43. Jesus speaking, **"I am come in my Father's name, and ye receive me not: If another shall come in his own name, him ye will receive."** The Jews are going to receive a future messiah, and he won't be Jesus Christ, unfortunately for them, but he will be the man of sin, the Antichrist. The Muslims will receive the 12th Imam they think, but, of course, it will be the Antichrist, and the Buddhists, the Maitreya, and any other group which you may want to consider. I would say that the Antichrist will cater for everybody. He will usher in world peace and CND and all the left-wing pressure groups and the climate-change people and "everything is okay" people. They're going to think this is wonderful – at last we've got peace. But Paul says then sudden destruction comes. So let's not even go down that road for now.

Go to Daniel, Daniel 11. And we need to understand that the Lord has given us many clear Scriptures and some not so clear. But the man of sin is actually found many, many times throughout the Bible. Look at verse 36, Daniel 11:36: **"And the king"** – he's called a king here – **"shall do according to his will; and he shall exalt himself, and magnify himself above every god"** – lower case "g" – **"and shall speak marvellous things against the God"** – capital "G" – **"of gods"** – lower case "g" – **"and shall prosper till the indignation be accomplished: for that that is determined shall be done. Neither** shall he regard the God of his fathers" – capital "G" – "nor the desire of women, nor regard any god: for he shall magnify himself above all."

I just want to stop there and say a few things. This bit of Scripture says that he will not regard the God of his fathers, and that is capital "G." This, for me, is probably the clearest indication that the Antichrist is going to be a Jew, and he's not going to regard the God of his fathers. He won't desire women either, and the Reformed crowd, the people who believe that the office of the papacy is the Antichrist, take this to be proof that the position of the papacy is found here because priests officially are not allowed to be married. Of course, many are married at all different levels from the papacy down to the parish priest, and the flip side of that is that a lot of priests are also homosexual around the world. So there is some credibility in that. But also on the Islamic side, people have said that this could be a reference to Muhammad because he didn't desire women, and because they use some of the newer Bibles where "G" is lower case "g," they can move it to Allah, the moon God. But if you let the text speak for itself – and I'm using the King James here – you will see that it is a reference to a Jewish person who doesn't prefer the God of his fathers.

I remember a priest that we met on the streets telling us that he thought that Muhammad was the Antichrist, rather interestingly. And I said to him, "Would you like to go on record and say that?" And he said, "Absolutely not." And I said to him before he scarpered off that his pope wouldn't have agreed with him, and his pope – I don't think it was John Paul II because it was a few years ago when we spoke to this priest – I said, "Does your pope kiss the Koran? And he wouldn't think that Muhammad was the Antichrist, but you think he was." That was interesting. Luther actually said that Muhammad was the firstborn of Satan, and, of course, he held to the office of the papacy being the Antichrist also.

Just a couple of more verses to look at in the 13th of Revelation. Fifteen, and we find the unholy trinity are still very much in power here. And it says here:

VERSE 15: "And he had power to give life unto the image of the beast, that the image of the beast should both speak, and cause that as many as would not worship the image of the beast should be killed."

Very much like Nebuchadnezzar.

VERSES 16-18: "And he causeth all, both small and great, rich and poor, free and bond, to receive a mark in their right hand, or in their foreheads: And that no man might buy or sell, save he that had the mark, or the name of the beast, or the number of his name. Here is wisdom. Let him that hath understanding count the number of the beast: for it is the number of a man; and his number is Six hundred threescore and six."

All right. A couple more things that I want to say, and then I'll close this clip. If you want to go down the Reformed route that the office of the papacy is the Antichrist, then what is this reference to of right hands and marks in the foreheads? Up to the last 10, 20, 30 years nobody was chipped in this country or in any country of the world. Now everyone is being chipped. Even members of the Royal Family, we're told, are chipped. Also, we have people living around the world that are not religious whatsoever, and they're able to buy and sell and live pretty happily, and there's no restrictions on them. And I go back to my overall theme with this video: If you're not a futurist, what are you? If you want to become a historicist, then how do you exegete these Scriptures? I'm sure you've got some responses for me on that. But I just go back to the original mindset that I have here that this has to be a reference to a future event, and I've yet to see anything that I've read or seen since I've been saved to explain Revelation any other way.

I just wanted to take a few moments out going through Revelation to deal with some of the usual arguments that are put against those of us that are into futurism that somehow we've been deceived by the Jesuits, and the reason I want to do this is because the allegation has long been around that to take the heat off the papacy being called Antichrist by Protestants around the world, the Jesuits, the society of Jesus, as they're called, were given the task to somehow take the spotlight off the papacy and put it onto a future man of sin. And this was done, it is alleged, by re-interpreting the Scripture to suggest that a future character will come on the scene, and this future character would be the Antichrist; and because some of us hold to futurism, we've somehow fallen prey to this elaborate Jesuit hoax.

Now, the reality is that most Christians in the UK don't hold to futurism. That's the first thing I want to say. Secondly, we always go to the Scripture. I was talking to a man on the street yesterday, I think it was, giving out tracts, and we were talking about many different subjects. And he was giving out his tracts and I was giving out my tracts, and he didn't believe in eternal security, and he said to me that the early 'fathers' didn't believe in eternal security. And I said to him, "You don't want to be going with the early 'fathers' because a lot of the early 'fathers' had some very strange views." I think it was Origen who mutilated himself in light of Matthew 5 because he couldn't stop lusting. Another 'father' said that Satan would be saved, and another one said that Jesus was inferior to the 'father.' So a lot of these early church leaders weren't as orthodox as we have been led to believe. Luther called them church babies. And I said to this chap, "We need to check everything in light of Scripture." Now, he didn't know about these 'fathers,' and whether or not he'll do his own research is not clear. But whether this is an elaborate hoax from the Jesuits or not is actually irrelevant because the Bible does teach a future man of sin, and if you saw the last video, you will know what I'm referring to.

Also, I want to say something else along this line that if we accept the allegation that we've somehow been deceived by powers that be, then I feel we do a great disservice to those that have gone before us. And I'm thinking of somebody like John Nelson Darby. For those that don't know, John Nelson Darby was a bishop in the church of Ireland, and he had an accident one day, and during his period of recuperation, he got into the Scriptures and discovered Bible prophecy, something which he had never really paid much attention to before; in fact, probably had no need to. No doubt he was raised with Replacement Theology and a-millennialism as most of these high churches are, and the more he got into the Bible, the more he realised the Rapture would occur before the Tribulation. He saw Jacob's trouble and a thousand year reign. Now, at the time we can't say that nobody had this belief, but we would argue that Darby rediscovered the Rapture and the thousand-year-reign.

Now, we know from church history that a man called Ephrem in the seventh century believed that Christ would come back for His church before the Tribulation, and there's a reference in his writings to being caught up – the church being caught up, I should say, and we certainly know that the early church leaders right up and including Eusebius held to a thousand year reign. But Eusebius left that belief and went off to a-millennialism. And Augustine, I think, was also a pre-millennial believer at one stage, but he too left it and took on the belief of a-millennialism. And I've touched on that briefly on another video which should be going on line pretty soon.

If we go back just a couple of hundred years prior to Darby, we have the backend of the Reformation, and we have Luther, Calvin, and some of the other guys rediscovering Sola Fide and Sola Scriptura. And I think what we can say with all honesty is bit by bit, generation by generation the Lord reveals more things to more people over a period of time. I remember talking to an old brother about the gap theory, and I personally am not swayed that there is a gap theory, but I'm probably on the fence. Persuade me if you will. But this brother put an interesting point across to me that the gap theory was discovered or rediscovered, as he would have it, during the time of Darwinism, and the gap theory does allow the earth to be older than it actually is. Now, personally, I don't think we need the gap theory to deal with Darwinism or even the age of the earth, but he was convinced that its rediscovery during the time of Darwin allowed the church at the time to deal with Darwinism. Now, like I say, I don't think we need it, but in his mind he was convinced that's what it was for; it was there for a purpose.

These guys, whether it's Darby or Luther or whatever, they did go through the Scriptures, and certainly in Luther's day, he was probably the first to really go through the Scriptures and find a whole lot of things which he'd never seen before. And I think it's also fair to say that Darby had been raised in the church system and had missed an awful lot of Bible. I know when I first got saved and I started to read the Bible, I was amazed at what I hadn't seen and didn't know. And I wasn't raised from a – or I hadn't come from a clerical background. I was just a member of the laity. But imagine the shock if you come from a clergy, clerical background and you are hearing all these things for the first time.

So what I want to say is this. Let's not give the Jesuits too much credit. It's easily done, and the Bible is going to be our final authority –it has to be. And if you're not going with the Scriptures, if you're not checking everything line by line, precept upon precept, then you may well buy into this Jesuit theory, and if you do, then it's your loss because there are two parts of eschatology which need to be kept in mind. Paul, for example, was writing to his initial audience, the New Testament churches, and he was also speaking to the church age which came on the backend of that, but he was also talking to those in the Tribulation. And let's not start slicing up the Scriptures and taking out bits here and bits there and eisegeting the Scripture when we should be exegeting the Scripture, and let's stop giving the Jesuits and the Dominicans and the flat-earthers and the vegetarians and the Hindus and the Buddhists and all the other guys any credit, and let's just stay with the Scripture, and the Lord will show us what He wants us to see.

I think it's worth reminding ourselves as to why the belief in a thousand year reign died out in the fourth century. If you can picture yourself living in a part of the world where the Catholic church is very much in control of everything and the priests are your mediators between Heaven and earth and you've got a belief, a system, a theory, a thought that one day the Jews, the chosen race would be grafted back into God's plan. Romans 11 says that the root is holy and we are the ones that are grafted in, and at the end of the fullness of the Gentiles, the Lord returns to Israel and grafts her back into His plan. But just imagine you're living in a Catholic country, like I said, back in the fourth, fifth century or even up to the Reformation and you've got people going around saying that any minute the Rapture is going to come and people are going to be caught up and the Tribulation will begin and a third of the Jews will be saved. It completely undermines the power and authority of the papacy. You see, in Roman Catholicism, the priest is the mediator between God and man. If there's no priest, then there's no Mass, and if there's no Mass, there's no salvation. So when people are threatened, when people feel that they're going to lose their power, they do dangerous things.

Look at John 11:47: **"Then gathered the chief priests and the Pharisees a council, and said, What do we? for this man doeth many miracles. If we let him thus alone, all men will believe on him: and the Romans shall come and take away both our place and nation."** So you can see that they are already of the opinion if the Lord continues His ministry that they will lose their nation. And, of course, that's not and that wasn't going to happen at the First Advent – the Second Advent, yes, but not the First Advent.

Look at 49: **"And one of them, named Caiaphas, being the high priest that same year, said unto them, Ye know nothing at all, Nor consider that it is expedient for us, that one man should die for the**

people, and that the whole nation perish not." So there you have a picture of the Lord dying for the whole nation of Israel – not just the elect – all of the people of Israel, and the nation didn't perish.

Fifty-one: **"And this spake he not of himself: but being high priest that year, he prophesied that Jesus should die for that nation; And not for that nation only, but that also he should gather together in one the children of God that were scattered abroad. Then from that day forth they took counsel together for to put him to death."** Now, simply understanding that the atonement is completely universal and without exception to those that believe on Him doesn't mean that everybody is going to be automatically saved. And we've made the case pretty conclusively in previous videos that you personally have to receive His forgiveness, which God has already granted to you through the preaching of the cross, and I may return to that on another occasion.

But like I say, this is the main reason that the leaders in Israel got together to put the Lord to death. Yes, blasphemy was part of it; yes, sedition was part of it; but the main reason, the main cause of it was they did not want to lose their power. And you find something very similar, as I say, throughout the minds and the councils in Rome throughout the Dark Ages. One of the reasons why the Inquisition took ground was they were very concerned that if they didn't stamp on it quick enough, people would become critical of Catholicism and look elsewhere for their salvation. By the time Luther was raised up, there was no going back. The Lord had clearly opened a door, and even the Catholic church with all her power, all her money, all her political connections wasn't able to stamp on Martin Luther. And we know that the Dukes and the leaders in Germany certainly protected him.

Also, it's similar to what we see in Geneva with John Calvin, and I've always found this whole area of Reformed Theology and the belief that God is going to switch from Catholicism to Protestantism – and there are many, many problems with Protestantism, and, again, on a future video, I'll take a look at that too. But I think the way that Geneva was set up was the council was the masters, if you will, and Calvin was their puppet leader. Calvin was very unpopular with a lot of people in Geneva. In fact, he was so unpopular, not only was he called a Protestant pope, but I also believe he was set up. I believe he was set up by people in Geneva and those on the council. And that's one of the reasons why Servetus turned up with some of his teachings which were contrary to Scripture. Nobody rejects that. He wasn't orthodox. He didn't believe in the Trinity or the eternal Sonship of Christ, and, yes, he also had an interest in astrology. But nonetheless, that didn't give the green light to those in Geneva to take his life. Again, I've done videos on all that, so I won't go over it again.

But Servetus was sent to Geneva on the understanding that he would be given some kind of safe haven. Nothing could be further from the truth. I think it's not too much of a stretch to look at Servetus and his beliefs, his theories as possibly undermining the position that the people of Geneva had taken. They wanted a reformed city of God, and I think John 11:52 to 53 comes into play. If you threaten any system, whether it's political or religious, certain groups within those systems will retaliate, and tragically for a lot of people – and we think since the fourth century up to the nineteenth century, around 50 million people died under the papacy, and most Catholics don't know that and most Protestants don't know that and, sadly, don't even care. But as it was once said, absolute power corrupts; power corrupts absolutely. And we've got to be so careful – all of us – if we ever come into a position of authority, a position of respect, that we don't let it go to our heads.

Okay. We looked at the Antichrist last time, and I do think that the Antichrist is a Jew. I know some people think it's a pope. Some people think it's going to be a Muslim, but I've always been of the mindset that it will be a Jew, and I look at John 5:43: **"I am come in my Father's name, and ye receive me not: if another shall come in his own name, him ye will receive."** The Jews rejected Christ at the First

Advent for many reasons, which leaves the Jews of today – the religious Jews, anyway – looking for His coming. Now, we've said in previous videos that the Messiah that the Jews, the unsaved, the apostate Jews will receive will be the Antichrist, and the Antichrist will be the 12th Imam, which the Muslims will go for, the Maitreya for the Buddhists, and probably the Freemasons, their great architect of the universe. All of these false views will all amalgamate into the Antichrist. And Matthew 24 says, if it were possible, even the elect would be deceived. But it's not possible and we give God the glory that it's not, because none of us are as holy and as righteous as we should be or like to think that we are.

Look at Acts 17:11: **"These were more noble than those in Thessalonica, in that they received the word with all readiness of mind, and searched the scriptures daily, whether those things were so."** Here you have a group of Jews who are checking everything that Paul tells them in light of the Old Testament. Paul is an apostle; he's been commissioned and sent from the Lord, and they are checking him out in light of Scripture. Wouldn't it be amazing if every Roman Catholic got their Bibles opened, even their Douay Rheims or their Jerusalem Bible, the Vulgate, whatever Bible they've got and opened it and checked out what the church taught them. And, of course, there are many problems with those Bibles. The Vulgate has many translational errors; the Douay Rheims pre-dates the King James Bible, and there's also a lot of textual problems with that. But the point I'm trying to make is, if they checked what they were taught in light of Scripture, those that were honest enough and weren't lazy enough would come to the realization that what they've been told about the Catholic church – the setup, the five-or six-tier system from the Pope right down to the parish priest and these intercessors from Mary to the saints – all the other problems with Catholicism would be completely brushed away, and they would realise from the word of God that their righteousness is as filthy rags, and without Christ, they are totally lost, completely in darkness.

CHAPTER 14 VERSE 1: "And I looked, and, lo, a Lamb stood on the mount Sion, and with him an hundred forty and four thousand, having his Father's name written in their foreheads."

I just want to stop there for a minute and add a quick comment. The 13th of Revelation, verse 1, the new Bibles have **"And he stood upon the sand of the sea,"** and they try and change the pronoun, which is referring to John when he says "I stood" to "he," referring to the devil, and that's a pretty twisted understanding of the Scripture, and it leads you down a very slippery path because once you start correcting the Bible, where do you end?

I've said it in the past and I'll say it again that if you are a medical student and you're at medical school, what would the chances be that you would be correcting your tutors? You've paid to be educated and to understand medicine, and you have to bow to your superiors. They are the ones that have the expertise and the information that you need. It's also fair to say that Muslims on the whole would never correct their Koran, and yet we've got Christians all over the world correcting the Bible. And I have to ask, where do they get the authority to do that from? Just imagine a young Christian gets saved and you've told them that they're saved by faith in Christ alone, and you've taken them through the Scriptures, and then six months down the line, they come across a great godly scholar who knows Greek and Hebrew – and there's nothing wrong with knowing Greek or Hebrew. Some people may have a phobia about Greek, Hebrew, and Aramaic, but that's not the issue. The issue is, what is your final authority? And you get a young Christian just saved, and he hears people correcting his Bible, and in the end he realises he has no final authority. These scholars are 'the final authority,' and to continue to get 'the final authority,' you have to go to their churches; you have to buy their books; you have to pay their seminary fees, and that's a really slippery road.

So I just wanted to point that out before I get into Revelation 14 because I'm thankful that I've got a lot of different Bible translations, but, for me, as an Englishman, my final authority will be the King James Bible, and the simplest and quickest way to answer that is the fact that it's based on the most superior manuscripts. And since, I think, it's 1881, we've had something like 75 Bibles come out, and every year they are trying to improve it, trying to get nearer to the original, and yet for 400 plus years we've had the King James Bible, and it's seen many, many people saved. It's been the bedrock of the British Empire – or what's left of it now – and you have to wonder who is behind all these attacks on the AV. And I know who I think it is, but maybe we will talk about that on another occasion.

Okay. Now, here you have the Lamb standing on Mount Zion and He's got 144,000 with him, and they've got the name of their Father written in their foreheads. Go to Isaiah 24, Isaiah 24:23: **"Then the moon shall be confounded, and the sun ashamed, when the LORD of hosts shall reign in mount Zion, and in Jerusalem, and before his ancients gloriously."** Look at that word **"LORD"** – capital "L," capital "O," capital "R," capital "D" – a reference to Jehovah God. And yet in Revelation John tells you it's the Lamb, and the Lamb of God is the Son of God, not God the Father. So Scripture with Scripture. And we see that not only is Jesus Christ God Almighty, but He's going to come and reign in Mount Zion.

Now, some people look at Revelation 14 as a reference to the mid-trib Rapture, and there's no doubt that the Lord has come back to earth at this stage with His Jewish evangelists – and we'll get to that in a minute – but because the book of Revelation isn't necessarily in chronological order, you could easily read this and have it at the end of the Tribulation before He goes into the millennial reign. So I just wanted to share that point with you.

VERSES 2-3: "And I heard a voice from heaven, as the voice of many waters, and as the voice of a great thunder: and I heard the

voice of harpers harping with their harps: And they sung as it were a new song before the throne, and before the four beasts, and the elders: and no man could learn that song but the hundred and forty and four thousand, which were redeemed from the earth."

Now, as you go through Scripture, especially the book of Revelation building up to the final crescendo, you'll note that there are less and less people getting saved. Many people are being killed by the Lord, but the great harvest seems to be almost nonexistent.

VERSE 4: "These are they which were not defiled with women; for they are virgins. These are they which follow the Lamb whithersoever he goeth. These were redeemed from among men, being the firstfruits unto God and to the Lamb."

The Jehovah's Witnesses believe they are the 144,000. Not all JWs will be privileged, they would have you believe, to be among the 144,000, but they want to attain to be in that special group of people. But it's not speaking about Jehovah's Witnesses; it's speaking about male virgin Jews, 12,000 from each of the 12 tribes. And just a bit of Scripture, and you'd be amazed what you can learn.

Also, just a quick footnote. The Mormons believe in the book of Ezekiel when it speaks about the tribe of Joseph, they honestly believe that is a reference to Joseph Smith, their founder and god. But, of course, it's not referring to Smith. He was a Gentile, by the way; he wasn't even a Jew. But it's a reference to the tribe of Joseph. And you get into British Israelism and all the other schisms and heretical groups out there which, once again, are trying to steal promises in the Jewish Bible to the Jewish people. And, again, this is a Tribulation book, and the Tribulation is for the Jews, not for the church.

VERSE 8: "And there followed another angel, saying, Babylon is fallen, is fallen, that great city, because she made all nations drink of the wine of the wrath of her fornication."

Now, we've looked at Jezebel earlier on in Revelation, and we'll get to Chapter 17 and 18 and 19 in a few videos' time. But here you have a picture of Babylon, the great city. She's fallen, and she's made all the nations drink of the wine of the wrath. There are two views to the reference of Babylon. The first view has it being ancient Iraq with a greater fulfilment in future Iraq, and as of 2010, Iraq is still in a very precarious state. All of the British troops have withdrawn from Iraq, and there's probably a very small battalion or two battalions of soldiers training Iraqi forces, but at the height of the Iraq war, Britain had about 48,000 soldiers there, and I think in total, 150-to 200,000 went through Iraq. America still has about 100,000 troops there, and by the end of Obama's first term, he hopes to have all the troops out of Iraq.

However, America has built the largest embassy in the world – I believe reports had it initially at 5,000 US staff from the State Department are going to be based in Iraq, and the embassy was just outside of Babylon. Very interesting.

But even if all that is kept in mind, as of today and as of fifty years ago and a hundred years ago, it's very difficult to think of Babylon being this great city which John is looking at from 90 AD. The second view, of course, is that it's a reference to Rome. Rome, of course, was what the Reformers understood Babylon to be. And there's two parts of that. The first position is the spiritual Rome where, of course, the Pope, the Bishop of Rome lives, but there's also a political Babylon, and a lot of people consider political Babylon to be in New York in America. And maybe we'll get to that as we go on.

VERSES 9-11: "And the third angel followed them, saying with a loud voice, If any man worship the beast and his image, and receive his mark in his forehead, or in his hand, The same shall drink of the wine of the wrath of God, which is poured out without mixture into the cup of his indignation; and he shall be tormented with fire and brimstone in the presence of the holy angels, and in the presence of the Lamb: And the smoke of their torment ascendeth up for ever and ever: and they have no rest day nor night,

who worship the beast and his image, and whosoever receiveth the mark of his name."

There is no annihilation when a person dies. If an unsaved man dies today, he goes into the ground and he has experienced the first death. The King James translates that place as Hell, and a lot of people have a problem with that and they say it should be Hades. But nonetheless, Hell is where he is; it's under your feet. And if you want to get into name calling and the terms for the departed dead, just go into any building site and start saying, "What the Hades did you do last night?" It makes no sense, of course. But if you say, "What the Hell did you do last night," they know what you mean. There's something very powerful about the word "Hell," and there's nothing worse than when you hear children use that word in a loose way.

A couple of things I want to say. People that believe in conditional security will say in verse 9 that if a saved person takes the mark of the beast, they're going to go to Hell. No. For me, that would be the equivalent of saying if you're a saved person and you start reading the Koran, for example, and then you say, "Allah is the only God," then you go to Hell, well, clearly if that were the case, then you're not a Christian; you never were a Christian. You may have had an experience; you may have had some manifestation, but you were never actually bone of His bone and flesh of His flesh.

Now, you can apostatise – and I've already given you 1 John 2 – and those that apostatise and never come back to the Lord were never His in the first place. But if you are the Lord's and you fall into a sin for a season, then you'll always come back to the Lord. But even if you don't come back to the Lord, that's no evidence that you weren't one of His in the first place. Paul speaks about the Corinthians, a very carnal, depraved church. In fact, there's a man in Corinth who's sleeping with his father's wife, his biological mother, and there's every reason to believe that his father is also sleeping with the same woman. Paul says it wasn't even named among the Gentiles. And bear this in mind, this is first century Corinth, a godless, depraved part of the Roman Empire. You had female prostitutes on tap 24/7. So for Paul to say it wasn't even spoken about among the Gentiles means that this really was a serious, wicked, depraved man from a very wicked family. Now, I'm not saying they were sharing her at the same time, but they were both sleeping with her. I mean, you can use your own imagination here.

But the point I'm trying to make is, here's a man who has completely fell into sin, and Paul says, "Put him out of your church." Now, he doesn't say the man isn't saved; he says, "Put him out." And in other Scriptures he says, "Treat these people like your brother," but they are put out of the assembly, and Satan will destroy the flesh that the spirit may be saved in the day of the Lord.

One other point I want to mention. During the Gulf War of 2003 we had Anglican vicars that were sent out to the war zone as chaplains, and a prayer was written up by the Ministry of Defence and no doubt supported by the Foreign and Commonwealth Office that if an Anglican vicar came across a dying Iraqi soldier, he would pray the prayer that Muslims say before they die along the lines that "There's no God but Allah." And, for me, as a Bible-believing Christian, I find it absolutely shocking that a so-called Christian would pray that sort of a prayer with a dying Muslim – much like Mother Teresa wouldn't criticise dying Hindus but she said she wanted to make them better Hindus. And you can see the mess that these ecumenical interfaith churches get into. Jesus says nobody comes to the Father but through Him. It is an exclusive ticket to Heaven. People then say, "Well, what about all the crowd that haven't heard of Jesus Christ?" And I always respond by saying, "Never mind those that haven't heard; how about those that have heard?"

Everybody in the UK who is of age knows who Christ is, and that would include America, Canada, probably the whole of the western world and even most parts of Africa, India, the Far East, Austria, Asia and beyond. What people are trying to do is get the heat off them and use some hypothetical scenario of a person who lives in a rain forest, has never heard of Christ, dies and goes to – they won't have him going to Hell because they don't want to believe that he dies and he goes somewhere, but because he didn't know who Christ was, he can't go to Hell. That's absolutely ludicrous. You go to Hell because you're a sinner, and your conscience tells you when you sin. And I'll say this: If you wanted to get saved, you could have got saved. I guarantee you, if you live in a village in India and you want to get saved, there will be somebody in the next village who knows somebody who can get you saved. There's always going to be somebody somewhere who can come to you and give you the full plan of salvation and even disciple you and get you on your feet. So let's not go down this road of people using hypothetical scenarios to simply get out of the fact that they're going to die and they will be judged without exception.

VERSE 12: "Here is the patience of the saints: here are they that keep the commandments of God, and the faith of Jesus."

We've looked at this on other videos. The commandments, according to 1 John 3, will be to believe on the Son of God, which is what gets you saved in the first place, and to love one another, to love your fellow brother. You're also told to love your enemies and pray for those which spitefully use you. So it's not that we just pray for each other and we never mix with non-Christians. No. We have to go out into the world. We have to be witnesses and lights to lost people to reflect the nature of God. And I will maybe come back to that subject, which will tie in with hyper-Calvinism, on another video.

Okay. Chapter 15. I'm not going to read all the verses in 15. I'm just going to pick out a few and add a few thoughts as I go through it.

CHAPTER 15

VERSE 2: "And I saw as it were a sea of glass mingled with fire: and them that had gotten the victory over the beast, and over his image, and over his mark, and over the number of his name, stand on the sea of glass, having the harps of God."

I just want to say a couple of things. There is this notion – and I've seen quite a few of these futuristic films. Tim LaHaye did the "Left Behind" series, and there was another video I think I watched with Mr. T from the A-Team, and apparently he's a Christian – you wouldn't think so, but apparently he is – and the theme of these films was that in the Tribulation there's going to be these hit squads going around trying to take out the Antichrist. And you've seen too many Hollywood films, because it's not going to happen that way. The Scripture says to resist the devil and he will flee from you (Js. 4:7.) The only way you're going to get victory over the beast in the Tribulation is through faith in the Son of God and staying close to the Lord and staying in the Scriptures. You can't in your own strength deal with a supernatural being like the devil, and if you're one of those people that thinks you can, then you've got another think coming. In fact, if you're one of those people that think you can bind the devil and rebuke the devil, let me take you to Jude, because we've got a lot of this loosing and binding going on in a lot of these churches.

Nine, Jude 9: **"Yet Michael the archangel"** – and here's an archangel, far more powerful than anybody else on this earth is – **"Michael the archangel, when contending with the devil he disputed about the body of Moses, durst not bring against him a railing accusation, but said, The Lord rebuke thee."**

Now, how is it that an archangel arguing with the devil over the body of Moses doesn't have the audacity, I suppose would be the right word, to rebuke Satan, and yet we've got people in Charismatic and Pentecostal churches all over the world talking to the devil, rebuking the devil, even writing books about the devil. We've got exorcists in the Vatican claiming to have done exorcisms on one another. I mean, it's such a screwed-up position of authority and theology here. You were told to resist the devil, and all this nonsense about casting out devils and other stuff like that is simply a delusion.

And I'll just say one other thing. When we go through the epistles, we get a very clear understanding that the Christian, the most important thing for that person is to be found bearing the fruits of the Spirit. So many books are written about the gifts of the Spirit, but look at Galatians 5:22. Fruits of the Spirit would be love, joy, peace, longsuffering, gentleness, goodness, faith, meekness, temperance, and he says, **"against such there is no law."** Now, why is it that we rarely hear anything about the fruits of the Spirit? And I think the honest truth is because such talk of the fruits does nothing to sell books. People want to be entertained. They read the book of Acts, and they want to experience some of the great events that the apostle Paul and Peter did. I mean, who wouldn't want to have the ability to heal sick children, go into a hospital ward and lay hands on everybody and heal the sick? In fact, I'll say this: Reading through the Gospels very carefully, it wasn't always the case that everybody was healed due to their own faith. People were healed in spite of their faith. In fact, if you go to Acts – and I haven't finished with Revelation.

If you go to Acts 2, I think it's Acts 2 – make it 3, verse 1: **"Now Peter and John went up together into the temple at the hour of prayer, being the ninth hour. And a certain man lame from his mother's womb was carried, whom they laid daily at the gate of the temple which is called Beautiful, to ask alms of them that entered into the temple"** – This guy wants money; 3, **"Who seeing Peter and John about to go into the temple asked an alms. And Peter, fastening his eyes upon him with John, said, Look on us. And he gave heed unto them, expecting to receive something of them."** Again, he's looking for money, this man. Look what Peter says: **"Silver and gold have I none; but such as I have give I thee: In the name of Jesus Christ of Nazareth rise up and walk. And he took him by the right hand, and lifted him up: and immediately his feet and ankle bones received strength."**

Now, here's a man who wasn't looking to be healed; he was looking for a handout, and the apostles through the gift of the Holy Spirit healed this man. And there's other occasions as the boy from Nain which the Gospel of Luke talks about. There was even Lazarus who had been dead for four days. He had no faith to be healed. And, again, the guy is healed immediately, and he's up and he's leaping and praising God in verse 8. And there's another verse which sometimes gets quoted by these people –11: **"And as the lame man which was healed held Peter and John, all the people ran together unto them in the porch that is called Solomon's, greatly wondering."** And some Charismatics will say, "Well, he healed this person or that person, and yet he's still hobbling around," and they somehow use verse 11 to justify it. Well, in 11, he's just got on his feet; he's dancing around; he's praising Peter and John, and the crowd came running towards him. He's actually hanging onto them for some kind of support. He's – I'll say this again. Verse 8 says he's leaping and praising God. So you don't get these types of healings anymore. What you get are people inviting you to go into their church.

I'll tell you a quick story, and we'll get back to Revelation.

I remember doing some street ministry, and this guy came over to me from the Full Gospel Business Men's Fellowship. And it all started out very well, and sooner or later we got on to theology and doctrine, which is what the Bible is written for. It says all Scripture was given by inspiration of God for reproof, for correction, for doctrine. So we can't get around it. We need the doctrine to be straight; otherwise, we could all be in error. And I got to talking to this man, and he said that the gifts of the Spirit were still for today. And I said to him, "Well, I beg to differ." I said, "I'm a cessationist," and I explained that to him. And he then looked rather surprised at me. And I said to him, "And also your movement, the Business Men's Fellowship, is ecumenical and hyper-charismatic. You believe in slaying in the spirit; you believe in the Toronto Blessing and all the usual crowd – Todd Bentley, Benny

Hinn and so on and so forth." And I said to him, "If you have the gift of healing, there's a blind man just fifty, a hundred yards from where we are standing. He's here all the time. As far as I can recall, he's always been blind. Why don't you go and lay hands on this man?" And he looked at me slightly bemused by my challenge, and I said to him, "He doesn't need to have faith to be healed, but he may have faith, I don't know." And he said to me, "Well, we wouldn't heal him on the street. We would expect him to come to our church, and then we'd all lay hands on him." And I said to him, "Listen, the early church did their healing on the street" – and I've just given you Acts Chapter 3 – "outside the Temple. Jesus did nothing in a corner."

So you get involved with these Pentecostals and Charismatics. You know, it all starts out very well with them, but their veneer soon falls off the minute you get into the theology and the doctrine, which is absolutely essential, because without that, you've got nothing. You know, we can all think that we're right, but the Bible says our hearts are desperately wicked, and even good people like Peter, he fell into sin, and it took the apostle Paul to publicly rebuke him in front of the whole church. So none of us are exempt from this.

CHAPTER 15

VERSE 3: "And they sing the song of Moses the servant of God, and the song of the Lamb, saying, Great and marvellous are thy works, Lord God Almighty; just and true are thy ways, thou King of saints."

Now, again, this is a Jewish book. This is a picture of the Jews coming out of Egypt; they've escaped Pharaoh, and he's been destroyed in the great flood and a similar picture to the Jews that are being saved in the Tribulation.

VERSE 4: "Who shall not fear thee, O Lord, and glorify thy name? for thou only art holy: for all nations shall come and worship before thee; for thy judgments are made manifest."

Again, this is a future time. People that get saved today are individuals, not nations.

VERSE 8: "And the temple was filled with smoke from the glory of God, and from his power; and no man was able to enter into the temple, till the seven plagues of the seven angels were fulfilled."

Now, you have like a reflection. Something is happening in Heaven which is happening on earth. Revelation 12 spoke about the dragon fighting with Michael as the man child was to be delivered. Now, it's very difficult to understand this – and I'm not sure that we can understand it – but you go to Matthew 18. This is a bit of Scripture which the Catholic church loves to quote, 18:18: **"Verily I say unto you, Whatsoever ye shall bind on earth shall be bound in heaven: and whatsoever ye shall loose on earth shall be loosed in heaven. Again I say unto you, That if two of you shall agree on earth as touching any thing that they shall ask, it shall be done for them of my Father which is in heaven. For where two or three are gathered together in my name, there am I in the midst of them."**

Now, whatever the apostles did on earth was agreed on in Heaven. Although in the context this is speaking about church discipline, the Lord gives the go-ahead for just two or three meeting in the name of Christ to be there to affirm what they do. In fact, if you go to 2 Corinthians 2:6 – make it 10, 2:10: **"To whom ye forgive any thing, I forgive also: for if I forgave any thing, to whom I forgave it, for your sakes forgave I it in the person of Christ; Lest Satan should get an advantage of us: for we are not ignorant of his devices."** So you get a very similar theme here that where two or three gather to forgive a person,

Paul says He's there with them in Spirit.

CHAPTER 16

VERSE 3: "And the second angel poured out his vial upon the sea; and it became as the blood of a dead man: and every living soul died in the sea."

There are some writers that believe that the book of Revelation is speaking about a local event around Israel, and others speak about it being a more general judgment. But my understanding of Revelation is that it's speaking about a universal judgment of men that are still on the earth.

VERSE 4: "And the third angel poured out his vial upon the rivers and fountains of waters; and they became blood."

Again, like Moses did with the Pharaoh on the River Nile.

VERSES 5-6: "And I heard the angel of the waters say, Thou art righteous, O Lord, which art, and wast, and shalt be, because thou hast judged thus. For they have shed the blood of saints and prophets, and thou hast given them blood to drink; for they are worthy."

Verse 6 is an interesting Scripture. It says, **"they have shed the blood of saints and prophets."** Who's "they"? Who are the saints and prophets? Who killed the New Testament saints and the early prophets? Was it Babylon in Iraq? Or was it Rome in Italy?

VERSE 7: "And I heard another out of the altar say, Even so, Lord God Almighty, true and righteous are thy judgments."

VERSE 9: "And men were scorched with great heat, and blasphemed the name of God, which hath power over these plagues: and they repented not to give him glory."

Now, here's a devastating indictment of man's wickedness. Throughout the Tribulation, the Gospel is being preached. You have the 144,000 going around. They've been trying to avoid the Antichrist; they've been trying to avoid the plagues, the vials to give people the chance to repent, and yet time and time, the Lord's mercy is thrown back in His face.

VERSES 10-11: "**And the fifth angel poured out his vial upon the seat of the beast**" – again, that's an expression for his power base – "**and his kingdom was full of darkness; and they gnawed their tongues for pain, And blasphemed the God of heaven because of their pains and their sores, and repented not of their deeds.**"

Here's a reference to unsaved people literally biting their tongues due to the pain. It's bad enough going to the dentist and having a tooth out or having a filling. I've never had a tooth taken out, but I've had fillings, and it's not very nice. But you've got a massive amount of heat, pains, and sores going on here. Again, Job is a typical picture of a Jew in the Tribulation, and here you've got people that will not bend the knee to the Lord.

VERSE 12: "**And the sixth angel poured out his vial upon the great river Euphrates; and the water thereof was dried up, that the way of the kings of the east might be prepared.**"

Now, a lot has been said about this. Is it the Chinese or the Russians? I will say this that you've got Israel as of 2010 just shy of 7 million Jews, some Arab Jews, some Messianic Christians; but nonetheless, just under 7 million people, and they are surrounded by 200 million Muslims. And I don't think much is going to change between now and the Second Advent. So I think if I was put on the spot, these kings of the East could easily come from Iran. In fact, we know that 40 percent of the Russian army as of this particular time is Muslim, and in the next 20 years, it's going to be 80 percent. And Muslims are divided on many points, but one thing they are all united on is their hatred of the Jews.

VERSE 13: "**And I saw three unclean spirits like frogs come out of the mouth of the dragon**" – of course, that's the devil – "**and out of the mouth of the beast**" – that's the Antichrist – "**and out of the mouth of the false prophet.**"

And I believe that is reference to the pope, a future pope – Pope Peter II, quite possibly – and according to Saint Malachy, he is going to be the antipope and the last pope. And I only give you that information because it's very much a talking point in Catholic eschatological circles because Catholics do believe in the Second Coming. They don't understand it particularly well, but they do believe that the age is going to end and there will be a great period of apostasy.

VERSE 14: "For they are the spirits of devils, working miracles, which go forth unto the kings of the earth and of the whole world, to gather them to the battle of that great day of God Almighty."

Scripture speaks about a time in the Old Testament when the Lord gathers the sons of God together – again, it's in Heaven – and there's a lot of evil on the earth; and a lying spirit comes forward, and the Lord uses that lying spirit to deceive wicked man. And the Lord will do that. I've said it time and time before, if your heart isn't right with the Lord, He will personally deceive you. Look at Pharaoh. Pharaoh started out with a hardened heart. He was a pagan; he was an idolater. And then the Lord hardens his heart; then he softens his heart, and the Lord hardens it again – it's a sort of cat-and-mouse game. But the point is that Pharaoh's heart was wrong to begin with.

The Lord doesn't harden saved people's hearts. He doesn't set out to destroy people for the fun of it, but He will humble people. If you're a saved person and you're in sin, He'll chastise you, according to Hebrews, and if you continue to sin, then your flesh will be destroyed, and that normally comes from excommunication and you're put out into the world system completely cut off from any kind of fellowship. But we shan't get into that now.

But by 14, these lying spirits of devils are going to go into the whole world and gather the kings to come against Israel. And, again, just look at the news. Look at the prophecy websites. You can see which nations at the moment are against little old Israel.

VERSE 15: "Behold, I come as a thief. Blessed is he that watcheth, and keepeth his garments, lest he walk naked, and they see his shame."

Imminency is the paramount interpretation from this. We don't know when the Rapture is going to come, and we are told to be ready in season and out of season to witness to people but also that we don't lose our reward. The Second Advent we know comes at the end of seven years, so in theory, the Rapture could come today, July 2010, and then you've got seven years of Tribulation. It may not come straightaway, but in theory, it could come soon after the Rapture, and then Christ comes back to the earth and we go into the thousand-year reign. You'd have signs that would point to that, but with the Rapture, we have no specific signs. We don't know when the Rapture will come. All that we do know is it could come any moment. And, like I said, Mark 13 told us to watch and wait.

VERSES 16-17: "And he gathered them together into a place called in the Hebrew tongue Armageddon. And the seventh angel poured out his vial into the air; and there came a great voice out of the temple of heaven, from the throne, saying, It is done."

It's completed. Jesus on the cross, John 19, He said it is done; it's finished. He's paid the price. He's atoned for the sins of the world. This is similar language. This is now moving to the final play-out of the Great Tribulation, God's judgment on a wicked world.

VERSES 18-20: "And there were voices, and thunders, and lightnings; and there was a great earthquake, such as was not since men were upon the earth, so mighty an earthquake, and so great. And the great city was divided into three parts, and the cities of the nations fell" – There's your capitals – **"and great Babylon came in remembrance before God, to give unto her the cup of the wine of the fierceness of his wrath. And every island fled away, and the mountains were not found."**

Has this happened yet? If you're not a futurist and you're a historicist, when did this happen? Please send me an email.

VERSE 21: "And there fell upon men a great hail out of heaven, every stone about the weight of a talent: and men blasphemed God

because of the plague of the hail; for the plague thereof was exceeding great."

Some people have said that had these events already occurred, the news organisations wouldn't have reported it; there would have been an order to cover it up, which is possible. We can't dismiss that. But if this happened, say, 500 years ago or a thousand years ago, we would have had church historians to write it down, and there's nothing in church history to suggest these things have happened yet. And I just say once more that if you're not a futurist, what do you do with these Scriptures?

CHAPTER 17 VERSE 1: "And there came one of the seven angels which had the seven vials, and talked with me, saying unto me, Come hither; I will shew unto thee the judgment of the great whore that sitteth upon many waters:"

This expression **"great whore"** obviously is feminine, and it's referring to not a literal woman, I believe, but an organisation in the feminine. For example, the Catholics will say 'Holy Mother Church,' as do the Greek and Russian Orthodox. It's not so much used in Protestant circles but more in Catholic and Orthodox circles. And, of course, that expression "many waters" we'll come back to in a minute.

VERSE 2: "With whom the kings of the earth have committed fornication, and the inhabitants of the earth have been made drunk with the wine of her fornication."

The kings of the earth would be quite obvious – the leaders, religious and also secular. And this expression **"have been made drunk with the wine of her fornication,"** again, I don't think this is a literal sexual fornication but a spiritual fornication; in other words, she's intoxicated these kings with her own system; and, of course, to be indoctrinated and intoxicated and deceived would mean to me that they were already deceived to start with.

VERSE 3: "So he carried me away in the spirit into the wilderness: and I saw a woman sit upon a scarlet coloured beast, full of names of blasphemy, having seven heads and ten horns."

Once again, John has been transported. He was on Patmos. Now he's in the spirit going into the wilderness, a bit like we find in Matthew 4 and Luke 4 when Christ goes into the wilderness to fast. This beast is scarlet, which, of course, would be the colour of the cardinals of Rome. They like to wear scarlet, as do the popes. It has the names of blasphemy, many names, which we'll find in verse 5. Seven heads and ten horns, we'll get to that a little later.

VERSE 4: "And the woman was arrayed in purple and scarlet colour, and decked with gold and precious stones and pearls, having a golden cup in her hand full of abominations and filthiness of her fornication:"

Now, when you go back through history, whether it's religious or secular, the list of people that this could be referring to narrows down, once again, to a particular organisation, and as we keep on going down, you'll see pretty soon who this is referencing to.

VERSE 5: "And upon her forehead was a name written, MYSTERY, BABYLON THE GREAT, THE MOTHER OF HARLOTS AND ABOMINATIONS OF THE EARTH."

Interesting it's on her forehead, a bit like the mark of the beast which we find in earlier chapters.

VERSE 6: "And I saw the woman drunken with the blood of the saints, and with the blood of the martyrs of Jesus: and when I saw her, I wondered with great admiration."

Now, keep this in mind that John the apostle had lived under Roman occupation his entire life as had all the apostles, and there's no doubt that he could quite possibly have gone to Rome throughout his long life, especially post the cross, and we know that Caesar's household had saved people. But here he looks with great admiration at this future Babylon, this future system which clearly hasn't yet come on the scene, which we'll find as we go a little further down. Also, it says that the woman was drunk with the blood of the saints. Now, this is – what? – 96 AD. He's looking into the future. And which organisation that sits on many waters has deceived the hierarchy of the world system and has the blood of the saints on her hands? Would you think it would be ancient Babylon in Iraq?

VERSE 7: "And the angel said unto me, Wherefore didst thou marvel? I will tell thee the mystery of the woman, and of the beast that carrieth her, which hath the seven heads and ten horns."

She sits on the beast, and here the beast is carrying her, so clearly these two are interlinked, and she becomes a prostitute in herself because she's living off the beast. And we'll find out a little bit more about this beast as we go on.

VERSE 8: "The beast that thou sawest was, and is not; and shall ascend out of the bottomless pit, and go into perdition: and they that dwell on the earth shall wonder, whose names were not written in the book of life from the foundation of the world, when they behold the beast that was, and is not, and yet is."

Once again, the Tribulation – especially this late part of Matthew 24, which would be the cross reference – is dealing with unsaved people. You won't get many saved people now. This is the final throw of the dice.

VERSES 9-10: "And here is the mind which hath wisdom. The seven heads are seven mountains, on which the woman sitteth. And there are seven kings: five are fallen, and one is, and the other is not yet come; and when he cometh, he must continue a short space."

Now, what a lot of Catholics will do when they get to this chapter, they'll say, well, this is a reference to ancient Rome. But like I've already said, the problem with that thinking is if it was ancient Rome, it wouldn't have been a shock for John because he had always lived under Rome. Just keep this in mind that the early church had lived under Rome all their life, and it was pagan Rome which killed all of the apostles except John. By the third and fourth or fifth century, pagan Rome has been replaced by religious Rome. That's not to say that pagan Rome wasn't religious; pagan Rome was very religious and superstitious and polytheist. But by the time of Constantine when Eusebius baptized him – and he was still an idolater; he still worshiped Vulcan, the sun god – but by the time of Constantine, Christianity, what was left of it from the biblical account, a true account of what Christianity should be, but what was left of Christianity by the time of Constantine was completely swept up and engrafted into pagan Rome. The popes replaced the Caesars and the cardinals replaced the Roman senate, and all of the statues and idols which had always been there replaced the saints. And you go to St. Peter's today, you've got all the statues of the apostles. In the old days, that would have been a reference to the old gods – Mercury, Jupiter, and all the other superstitious gods. So, again, a little bit of history, common sense, and an open mind, and the Holy Spirit will show you these things.

VERSE 11: "And the beast that was, and is not, even he is the eighth, and is of the seven, and goeth into perdition."

VERSE 12: "And the ten horns which thou sawest are ten kings, which have received no kingdom as yet; but receive power as kings one hour with the beast."

Now, again, this is futuristic, and I challenge anybody who's a historicist to tell me what these references mean to you. One hour is a figurative expression for a period of time, a very short period of time.

VERSE 13: "These have one mind, and shall give their power and strength unto the beast."

Again, this beast I think is a reference to the Antichrist – I'm pretty sure of it – and the powers to be are going to throw their lot in with him. But read on:

VERSES 14-15: "These shall make war with the Lamb, and the Lamb shall overcome them: for he is Lord of lords, and King of kings: and they that are with him are called, and chosen, and

faithful. **And he saith unto me, The waters which thou sawest, where the whore sitteth, are peoples, and multitudes, and nations, and tongues."**

Now, again, if you go to Rome today, you'll find it's a very mixed city of nations and tongues from all over the world. They call it the Eternal City, and, of course, the Eternal City is Jerusalem. But, once again, with replacement theology, the church of Rome has stolen another promise given to the Jews and adopted it for herself.

VERSE 16: "And the ten horns which thou sawest upon the beast, these shall hate the whore, and shall make her desolate and naked, and shall eat her flesh, and burn her with fire."

Okay. Now, by verse 16 the ten horns which sat upon the beast, the Antichrist – and the ten horns are the ten kings – are going to turn against the whore, which I believe is the Roman Catholic church, if you hadn't already guessed, and they are going to destroy her, which is quite remarkable because for 1400, 1600 years she's been a very powerful influence in the world. In fact, when any foreign leader goes to Italy, they always, always, always go into the Vatican and give the Pope a private briefing. And I've even heard accounts that when the Queen has gone to Stonyhurst – which is a Jesuit college, a Jesuit-run college in England – she not only wears black but she has to genuflect at the Jesuit superior. Now, I haven't had that confirmed, but I've heard that from more than one account, and I'd be very interested to know if you hear about that.

Also, please keep this in mind that verse 16, not only does the whore get destroyed, but all of the religious groups which are affiliated with her. And this is one of the reasons why we plead with Anglicans, Methodists, Baptists, Presbyterians, Protestants, any organisation that is in the ecumenical movement or is a part of the World Council of Churches, would you please come out of that organisation. We were talking to a brother, a friend of ours, just a couple of days ago, and he was doing some street ministry, and a Methodist minister took a tract from him. And these two got talking, and our friend told him that he was very concerned that this Methodist was in the ecumenical movement. And he said, "Well, we are trying to remove the Catholics from the ecumenical movement to have a Protestant ecumenical movement." Now, as far as I'm concerned, there's no real difference. They're both apostate. They both teach faith and works. They're both post-millennial. They're both trying to fix this broken world without getting people saved. But I thought, well, even if that was possible and they did remove the Catholics from the ecumenical movement, do you honestly think that they're going to preach against Rome? No, I don't think so.

VERSE 17: "For God hath put in their hearts to fulfil his will, and to agree, and give their kingdom unto the beast, until the words of God shall be fulfilled."

This is a stinging part of Scripture. These people are determined to do what they want to do, and the Lord has put it in their hearts to fulfil His will – much like Pharaoh, once again, and the Lord raised him up to destroy him. And here you have the kings and the beast working together to fulfil the Lord's will.

VERSE 18: "And the woman which thou sawest is that great city, which reigneth over the kings of the earth."

Once again, you give me any religious organisation in the world – Islam, Judaism, the Jehovah's Witnesses, the Mormons, the Moonies, the Scientologists – any organisation in the world and tell me which religion rules over the kings of the earth, which religion has the most respect given to her other than the Roman Catholic church. And when you can think of any organisation which comes anywhere near Roman Catholicism, please let me know.

CHAPTER 18

VERSES 1-2: "And after these things I saw another angel come down from heaven, having great power; and the earth was lightened with his glory. And he cried mightily with a strong voice, saying,

Babylon the great is fallen, is fallen, and is become the habitation of devils, and the hold of every foul spirit, and a cage of every unclean and hateful bird."

Of course, this is a reference to demons here.

VERSE 3: "For all nations have drunk of the wine of the wrath of her fornication, and the kings of the earth have committed fornication with her, and the merchants of the earth are waxed rich through the abundance of her delicacies."

It's also worth noting that the Catholic church has a seat at the United Nations, and she would refer to that as an observer, as do the Jehovah's Witnesses, by the way. It's not just the Catholics. But she has a seat at the United Nations, and she's also very interested in the European Union. So you can see how this amalgamation of political and secular leaders becoming one is going to play out further in the last days.

VERSE 4: "And I heard another voice from heaven, saying, Come out of her, my people, that ye be not partakers of her sins, and that ye receive not of her plagues."

Now, because all these churches – especially in the UK – are all inter-linked, when we look at verse 4, not only is it a reference to the whore on the seven hills, but it would be a reference to all of these false churches. And a large part of our ministry is to get Catholics saved and then help them to leave the Catholic system, because our experience has shown time and time again that it's not just the laity who are victims of Roman Catholicism; it's also many members of the clergy. A lot of the priests today who are in their 70s started in junior seminary when they were 12, 13, 14. That's all they've ever known. And there are a lot of priests who have come out of the Catholic church in the last 25 to 30 years, and we've also known of nuns that have come out. But we don't know of any bishops or cardinals that have come out, and I would say it's probably because they've got too much influence, and they've been given up [by God.]

But even in verse 4, the Lord says there are some of His people that are still in there, and He's desperately calling them out before the great judgment comes. And also 2 Corinthians 6:14 to 18 would come into play here that you're not to be yoked, you're not to be yoked in a spiritual sense to such organisations, and if you are yoked to these organisations, then you could receive of her plagues and not get a full reward.

VERSES 5-6: "For her sins have reached unto heaven, and God hath remembered her iniquities. Reward her even as she rewarded you, and double unto her double according to her works: in the cup which she hath filled fill to her double."

If you remember the earlier chapters we looked at in 6 and 7 when you've got the saints in Heaven that have been martyred and they're calling for judgment, and the Lord gives them their judgment. And you can see it's stepping up another gear here.

VERSES 7-8: "How much she hath glorified herself, and lived deliciously, so much torment and sorrow give her: for she saith in her heart, I sit a queen, and am no widow, and shall see no sorrow. Therefore shall her plagues come in one day, death, and mourning, and famine; and she shall be utterly burned with fire: for strong is the Lord God who judgeth her."

Again, it's the Lord God Himself who's going to judge this organisation. We're not interested in militias; we're not interested in people taking the law into their own hands. The God of the Bible, Jehovah God, will deal with this whore in His own way in His own time.

VERSES 9-10: "And the kings of the earth, who have committed fornication and lived deliciously with her, shall bewail her, and lament for her, when they shall see the smoke of her burning, Standing afar off for the fear of her torment, saying, Alas, alas, that great city Babylon, that mighty city! for in one hour is thy judgment come."

Now, some people refer to this as Babylon, and New York has been put forward. What I will say is that, when reading Scripture, you can sometimes get a dual application. And I gave you the reference in Matthew 24 when the Lord refers to the abomination of desolation and the Temple being surrounded, which is also in Luke's Gospel. And He's talking about 70 AD, but He's also talking about the Great Tribulation. So there's every possibility that Revelation 17 and 18 are split into two parts – religious Babylon and also secular Babylon. But look at verse 11:

VERSES 11-14: "And the merchants of the earth shall weep and mourn over her; for no man buyeth their merchandise any more: The merchandise of gold, and silver, and precious stones, and of pearls, and fine linen, and purple, and silk, and scarlet, and all thyine wood, and all manner vessels of ivory, and all manner vessels of most precious wood, and of brass, and iron, and marble, And cinnamon, and odours, and ointments, and frankincense, and wine, and oil, and fine flour, and wheat, and beasts, and sheep, and horses, and chariots, and slaves, and souls of men. And the fruits that thy soul lusted after are departed from thee, and all things which were dainty and goodly are departed from thee, and thou shalt find them no more at all."

Now, going back to Jeremiah just quickly. Jeremiah looks at Babylon as well, and here's a picture of the Jews in captivity in Babylon, which was, of course, ancient Iraq. And there's lots of parts of Jeremiah's account which is still futuristic. So you've got all these groups – Let's try and pull all of this together. You've got all of these groups. You've got Babylon, which was ancient Iraq, which in Revelation is referring to a future power base, which would be Roman Catholicism, but you've got all of the ecumenical groups in here. You've got the synagogue of Satan from Chapter 2 of Revelation; you've got the ecumenical movement, the interfaith; you've got all the political kings of the world and all of their baggage which they bring, all of their customs, and it's all being mixed up here, and it's inseparable.

And I think, really, what you need to keep in mind is that the way that the world system is run today, if you're not careful, you're going to be directly or indirectly yoked to these organisations. I mean, in the UK we have the Freemasons, which are pretty powerful still, but there's groups that feed into the Freemasons, so you have the Rotary Club. And not all Rotarians are Freemasons, but many of them are, and these are groups which, on the surface, do a lot of good works, claim to be making a difference in the community – and in some ways they are. They're building hospitals and doing good things. But it's the spiritual element which is behind a lot of these groups. The same is true of karate and taekwondo and all these martial arts sports. From a physical point of view, it looks all very interesting, but look at the spiritual element, the bowing down and the other aspects of it. And by the time we get to Revelation 18 – and I'm going back to Matthew 24 as a cross reference – you've got so much going on here that if it wasn't for the sake of the elect, everything would just go up in smoke.

VERSES 15-18: "The merchants of these things, which were made rich by her, shall stand afar off for the fear of her torment, weeping and wailing, And saying, Alas, alas, that great city, that was clothed in fine linen, and purple, and scarlet, and decked with gold, and precious stones, and pearls! For in one hour so great riches is come to nought. And every shipmaster, and all the company in ships, and sailors, and as many as trade by sea, stood afar off, And cried when they saw the smoke of her burning, saying, What city is like unto this great city!"

Now, has this already happened? And I keep making this point, but here is a massive city going up in smoke, and if it's already occurred, let me know which city it was. But my money is on this being a future account, not a past one.

VERSE 19: "And they cast dust on their heads, and cried, weeping and wailing, saying, Alas, alas, that great city, wherein were made rich all that had ships in the sea by reason of her costliness! for in one hour is she made desolate."

Now, we don't know all of the financial interests that the Catholic church has got their fingers in. I'm sure they've got connections the world over. We know that at least one or two dioceses in America are now bankrupt because of the paedophile payouts, and even in the UK they are struggling to find money to pay for the Pope's autumn visit. But they've had hundreds and hundreds of years to build up their wealth there and out of London too. And if you go to any capital city and there's a cathedral there, look at the land around the cathedral. There will be shops normally and houses and parks. Normally, not always but normally the Catholic church owns that as well. And I'll also say this: In the UK the largest landowner is actually the church of England, and their assets are worth about 5 billion pounds, and they've had years to build up this sort of power base.

VERSE 20: "Rejoice over her, thou heaven, and ye holy apostles and prophets; for God hath avenged you on her."

Now, again, who killed the apostles and prophets? Was it Babylon in Iraq or was it Rome in Italy?

VERSES 21-24: "And a mighty angel took up a stone like a great millstone, and cast it into the sea, saying, Thus with violence shall that great city Babylon be thrown down, and shall be found no more at all. And the voice of harpers, and musicians, and of pipers, and trumpeters, shall be heard no more at all in thee; and no craftsman, of whatsoever craft he be, shall be found any more in thee; and the sound of a millstone shall be heard no more at all in thee; And the light of a candle shall shine no more at all in thee; and the voice of the bridegroom and of the bride shall be heard no more at all in thee: for thy merchants were the great men of the earth; for by thy sorceries were all nations deceived. And in her was found the

blood of prophets, and of saints, and of all that were slain upon the earth."

That is why she falls down ultimately because her sorceries not only deceived her own people but it deceived the nations of the world. So I'm just going to close this Chapter and just give you one last historical point. Each of the Protestant church Reformers, as I've already said, not only adopted the twelfth century doctrine that the papacy was the Antichrist, but they all unanimously took Revelation 17 and 18 to be pointing to Babylon the Great, the great whore, being the Roman Catholic church. And we at this ministry, although we're not Calvinist, although we're not Protestant in the sense of ancient or historical Protestantism – and I want to do a video on that sometime soon – but nonetheless, we do affirm with the Reformers that the city and the great whore that rides the beast is the Roman Catholic church.

******

Okay. I just want to do a quick spin-off video in relation to the clips that I've been doing on Revelation. And we have almost nearly finished this series of clips, and I hope you've enjoyed them. But I just want to spend a few moments distinguishing the term **"many antichrists"** to "the Antichrist." In 1 John 2:18 the apostle John says, **"Little children, it is the last time"** – and that is a reference to probably the end of one dispensation going into another dispensation – **"and as ye have heard that antichrist shall come, even now are there many antichrists; whereby we know that it is the last time."** So there you have <u>an</u> Antichrist, the singular, and then you have many antichrists in the plural.

Go down to verse 22: **"Who is a liar but he that denieth that Jesus is the Christ? He is antichrist, that denieth the Father and the Son."** Now, when I look at verse 22, I think to myself, **"Which religion today denies that Jesus is the Messiah?"** And amazingly, it's not Islam. It's Judaism. The Jews do not believe that Christ is the Messiah of Israel.

They have a book called the Talmud which runs parallel to the Tanakh, the Old Testament, and in their Talmud they claim that the Lord Jesus Christ was a bastard who was conceived by a Roman soldier who raped the mother of the Lord Jesus Christ. And when you challenge them with this information, more often than not they won't admit it, but nonetheless it is found in their literature.

Verse 23: **"Whosoever denieth the Son, the same hath not the Father: (but) he that acknowledgeth the Son hath the Father also."** Which religion denies that Christ is the Son of God? Well, yes, the Jews deny Him, but so do the Muslims. And, once again, we find two groups of world religions that are falling into the category of antichrist, many antichrists, and you can go through Hinduism, Sikhism, Buddhism, and all the other world religions, and they all qualify to be classed as antichrist. But that is a distinction that has to be drawn from many antichrists in a general sense to a future Antichrist. And if you've been listening to these videos in Revelation, you'll see that we are narrowing down the list of candidates for the final Antichrist. The Vicar of Christ, a term which the Catholic church is quite fond of using, means another Christ, and the Greek word for antichrist means in place of Christ. And there are people who think that whenever you use the word antichrist it refers to somebody who is against Christ, and that's not the case at all. And if you translate *Vicarius Christi* into Greek, it comes out *antichristos*, antichrist. So, once again, a little bit of knowledge on languages does help.

But I do believe that even without the little bit of knowledge of Greek or Latin, you can still identify the main religious characters in the world today as being antichrist, and more often than not, it's not what they do but it's what they don't do. And when I look at photographs going back probably just prior to the Second Vatican Council and I see Pope Pius XII and John XXIII being carried around like kings, then I have to ask myself, "Do these people really believe that they are representing the Lord Jesus Christ?" He did say that he that was greatest among you should become your servant.

Even in modern times if you go to the Vatican today and you get an audience with Benedict XVI, you still are expected to show him reverence, and a lot of people will either kiss the ring or genuflect or bow down. And if you're a woman who has to visit the Pope and you're not a Catholic, you will be expected to wear black; and that, of course, is a reference to mourning because you are not a Catholic and you're in the presence of something holy, they would have you believe, and therefore to contrast his holiness, you have to be dressed in black. And even the Queen of England since the 60s has gone along with this Catholic protocol.

Just one final point, and we'll look at this in more detail on the next video. But with the way that the one-world religion and the ecumenical movement and the interfaith movement and the Freemasons and the Bilderbergers and all these groups, the way that these people are going, it is my belief that if you are a part of that setup, if you have aligned yourself with these groups and organisations, then it will be not only destroyed in the Tribulation, but it will be destroyed by the Antichrist amazingly, and it will be the Antichrist that these people will look to hoping and believing that he is their long-awaited Messiah, and he will turn and betray them – slightly similar to what we saw Judas Iscariot do. He was numbered among the twelve; he was anointed, sent out, did all the miracles. Christ knew what was going to happen, of course, but the apostles didn't know. Even Peter, the alleged first pope, didn't know that Judas was going to do what he did. Jesus didn't give him a briefing. And Judas, of course, arrives at the Garden of Gethsemane and betrays Jesus – a similar picture to what we're going to see from the Antichrist in the last days. In fact, I'll say this also that 2 Timothy 3:1 says, **"This know also, that in the last days perilous times shall come."**

And we're in those last days now. There won't be any more revivals. **"For men shall be lovers of their own selves, covetous, boasters,** proud, blasphemers, disobedient to parents, unthankful, unholy, Without natural affection, trucebreakers, false accusers, incontinent, fierce, despisers of those that are good, Traitors, heady, highminded, lovers of pleasures more than lovers of God; Having a form of godliness, but denying the power thereof: from such turn away."** And that is a very clear picture of the times that we are living in. Okay. Back to Revelation.

CHAPTER 19

VERSES 1-2: "And after these things I heard a great voice of much people in heaven" – again, there's no purgatory when you die. There's no going back into the ground – Hades, Sheol, Gehenna, Tarsus, whatever you want to call it. You die and you go straight to be with the Lord – **"saying, Alleluia; Salvation, and glory, and honour, and power, unto the Lord our God: For true and righteous are his judgments: for he hath judged the great whore, which did corrupt the earth with her fornication, and hath avenged the blood of his servants at her hand."**

Once again, these are the righteous dead from apostolic times right up to the end of the Tribulation.

VERSE 3: "And again they said, Alleluia – spelled with an "A" – **"And her smoke rose up for ever and ever."**

I've heard Muslims say this is a reference to Allah, and they try and lose the "e" and put an "a" there and mess around with the rest of the wording. But here you have the King James translation. And, of course, it is spelled with an "H" as well, but here it's translated with an "A." Back to 3:

VERSES 3-4: "And again they said, Alleluia. And her smoke rose up for ever and ever. And the four and twenty elders and the four beasts fell down and worshipped God that sat on the throne, saying, Amen; Alleluia."

These 24 elders have been suggested to be the 12 apostles and the 12 sons of Jacob, and I have no reason to doubt that. That seems to be the general consensus, anyway.

VERSES 5-7: "And a voice came out of the throne, saying, Praise our God, all ye his servants, and ye that fear him, both small and great. And I heard as it were the voice of a great multitude, and as the voice of many waters, and as the voice of mighty thunderings, saying, Alleluia: for the Lord God omnipotent reigneth. Let us be glad and rejoice, and give honour to him: for the marriage of the Lamb is come, and his wife hath made herself ready."

VERSE 8: "And to her was granted that she should be arrayed in fine linen, clean and white: for the fine linen is the righteousness of saints."

VERSES 9-10: "And he saith unto me, Write, Blessed are they which are called unto the marriage supper of the Lamb. And he saith unto me, These are the true sayings of God. And I fell at his feet to worship him. And he said unto me, See thou do it not: I am thy fellowservant, and of thy brethren that have the testimony of Jesus: worship God: for the testimony of Jesus is the spirit of prophecy."

There's absolutely no reason for anybody to fall down at another person's feet no matter how holy that person may or may not be. Only God is worthy of our worship.

VERSES 11-14: "And I saw heaven opened, and behold a white horse; and he that sat upon him was called Faithful and True, and in righteousness he doth judge and make war. His eyes were as a flame of fire, and on his head were many crowns; and he had a name written, that no man knew, but he himself. And he was clothed with a vesture dipped in blood: and his name is called The Word of God. And the armies which were in heaven followed him upon white horses, clothed in fine linen, white and clean."

Now, here you have a picture of the Lord leaving Heaven coming to earth, and we looked at this in the Rapture videos. Matthew 24, let's just go there quickly. Matthew 24 – I think it's 31. We have the Lord returning to earth with his armies, and, of course, you have the judgments from the 25th of Matthew. 31: **"And he shall send his angels with a great sound of a trumpet, and they shall gather together his elect from the four winds, from one end of heaven to the other."** He's simply going to accumulate all of the saved people wherever they are on the earth and usher them up to Jerusalem to go into the millennial reign.

Back to Revelation.

CHAPTER 19

VERSES 15-16: "And out of his mouth goeth a sharp sword, that with it he should smite the nations: and he shall rule them with a rod of iron" – again, Second Advent – **"and he treadeth the winepress of the fierceness and wrath of Almighty God. And he hath on his vesture and on his thigh a name written, KING OF KINGS, AND LORD OF LORDS."**

Now, He came at the first coming, and they mocked Him and spat at Him and nailed Him to a cross, and, of course, that's a reference to the son of Joseph. But here you see the Son of David coming back to claim the earth.

VERSES 17-18: "And I saw an angel standing in the sun; and he cried with a loud voice, saying to all the fowls that fly in the midst of heaven" – again, a reference to birds or even demons – **"Come and gather yourselves together unto the supper of the great God; That ye may eat the flesh of kings, and the flesh of captains, and the flesh of mighty men, and the flesh of horses, and of them that sit on them, and the flesh of all men, both free and bond, both small and great."**

This expression to eat flesh is also found in John 6, and the Catholic position is it's a literal rendering that you will physically eat the body of

Christ to be saved. And it's interesting because in John 6 it says that you have eternal life in the present tense, and yet Catholics don't believe in once saved always saved. It's an ongoing salvation and you have to keep coming back to church week after week and doing your penance and doing your rosaries and so on and so forth so you stay in fellowship with the Catholic system. Nothing here that you can argue would be used in a spiritual manner.

VERSE 19: "And I saw the beast" – Antichrist – **"and the kings of the earth, and their armies, gathered together to make war against him that sat on the horse, and against his army."**

You can see that the whore is now no more. It's the Antichrist's time to shine.

VERSES 20-21: "And the beast was taken, and with him the false prophet that wrought miracles before him, with which he deceived them that had received the mark of the beast, and them that worshipped his image. These both were cast alive into a lake of fire burning with brimstone. And the remnant were slain with the sword of him that sat upon the horse, which sword proceeded out of his mouth: and all the fowls were filled with their flesh."

Now, read this very carefully. You've got the Antichrist and the false prophet going into the lake of fire, and there's no annihilation because you've got 1000 years now where they're going to be burning. This isn't the second death, by the way; this is the first death. Luke 16 tells you what the first death entails – Read verses 19 to 31. And at the end of the thousand years, they are resurrected or brought up from Hell – the first death, not the second death – and, of course, they have their final day with the Lord. But you cannot get annihilation from Revelation 19.

CHAPTER 20

VERSE 1: "And I saw an angel come down from heaven, having the key of the bottomless pit and a great chain in his hand."

I just want to stop right there for a minute and point out the fact that this is just an angel, not the archangel; it's not Michael; it's not the Angel of the Lord, which was normally a Christophany, Christ pre-incarnate. This is <u>an</u> angel of the Lord. And just keep your finger in Revelation 20 and go back to Isaiah, Isaiah 14 verse 9: **"Hell from beneath is moved for thee to meet thee at thy coming: it stirreth up the dead for thee, even all the chief ones of the earth; it hath raised up from their thrones all the kings of the nations. All they shall speak and say unto thee, Art thou also become weak as we? art thou become like unto us? Thy pomp is brought down to the grave, and the noise of thy viols: the worm is spread under thee, and the worms cover thee. How art thou fallen from heaven, O Lucifer, son of the morning! how art thou cut down to the ground, which didst weaken the nations! For thou hast said in thine heart, I will ascend into heaven, I will exalt my throne above the stars of God: I will sit also upon the mount of the congregation, in the sides of the north: I will ascend above the heights of the clouds; I will be like the most High. Yet thou shalt be brought down to hell, to the sides of the pit. They that see thee shall narrowly look upon thee, and consider thee, saying, Is this the man that made the earth to tremble, that did shake kingdoms; That made the world as a wilderness, and destroyed the cities thereof; that opened not the house of his prisoners? All the kings of the nations, even all of them, lie in glory, every one in his own house."**

And you can read the rest of Isaiah 14. This is a reference to the devil, and this is the expression how the mighty fall. And in Revelation 20 verse 1 an angel, just an angel, an unnamed angel is given the task to go down and bind the dragon. Look at 2:

VERSES 2-3: "And he laid hold on the dragon, that old serpent, which is the Devil, and Satan, and bound him a thousand years, And cast him into the bottomless pit, and shut him up, and set a seal upon him, that he should deceive the nations no more, till the thousand years should be fulfilled: and after that he must be loosed a little season."

I just want to stop there and add another quick note on the Isaiah Scripture. Luke Chapter 16 verses 19 to 31 isn't a parable. It's a literal account of a man who died before Jesus came on the earth and died in his sins. And the dialogue between the rich man and Abraham is quite a fascinating and yet a very somber one because Abraham says to the man in Hell, as it were, that he had the prophets and Moses; in other words, he was accountable with the light that he had in his own generation. And today we have Christ; we have the Bible; we have it in multiple languages; we have online Bible translations. There are ministries all around the world which send out free Bibles, and it's going to be shocking when the Great White Throne comes around and all these people stand before Christ and they've got nothing whatsoever to say in their defence. They are more accountable than the man in Luke 16.

VERSE 4: "And I saw thrones, and they sat upon them, and judgment was given unto them" – cross reference this with 1 Corinthians 6 – **"and I saw the souls of them that were beheaded for the witness of Jesus, and for the word of God, and which had not worshipped the beast, neither his image, neither had received his mark upon their foreheads, or in their hands; and they lived and reigned with Christ a thousand years."**

The expression **"beheaded"** simply refers to the guillotine. And the guillotine hasn't been completely removed. I believe these guillotines are still in France to this day, and no doubt they're in museums around the world. But in the Tribulation they're going to be wielded out and used. And they were last used even in World War II, and I believe even in Soviet Russia they were used. Now, **"thousand years"** is going to appear three times, so look at it carefully.

VERSES 5-7: "But the rest of the dead lived not again until the thousand years were finished. This is the first resurrection. Blessed and holy is he that hath part in the first resurrection: on such the second death hath no power, but they shall be priests of God and

of Christ, and shall reign with him a thousand years. And when the thousand years are expired, Satan shall be loosed out of his prison,"

There's no annihilation here. The devil goes into Hell, and 1000 years later he's brought up and he gets one more chance to deceive the wicked nations. All of the saved Jews, if you go back to the Gospel accounts – and you get a picture of this in Matthew 27, I think it is. Let's just go there quickly. Jesus dies on the cross and He says, **"It is finished,"** and He goes into the grave, and on the third day the triune God raises Him from the dead. John 2 says the Son raises Himself from the dead; Galatians 1 has the Father raising Him from the dead; and Romans 11 has the Holy Spirit raising Him from the dead.

Yes, Matthew 27:52: **"And the graves were opened; and many bodies of the saints which slept arose, And came out of the graves after his resurrection, and went into the holy city, and appeared unto many."** Now, that's all we get, just those two verses. The way I understand this to be is this is a picture obviously of the saved people that are going to go up in the Rapture with the Lord. And you go to Ephesians and Colossians, it says that Jesus went into the lower parts of the earth, scooped up those that were saved and took them up to Heaven, and we've just seen from the 19th Chapter of Revelation that the armies leave Heaven with the Lord.

So at the Second Advent – not the Rapture but the Second Advent – Christ comes back to the earth with all of the Old Testament saved Jews, all of the church-age saints and, of course, the Tribulation saints. All of the others, all of the unsaved dead are going to stay in the ground, according to Luke 16, burning in flames until the Great White Throne comes upon them.

VERSES 8-9: "And shall go out to deceive the nations" – this, of course, is Satan – **"which are in the four quarters of the earth, Gog and Magog, to gather them together to battle: the number of whom is as the sand of the sea. And they went up on the breadth of the earth, and compassed the camp of the saints about, and the beloved**

city: and fire came down from God out of heaven, and devoured them."

This clearly was a suicide mission, and the Lord knew it, the devil knew it, but whether those unsaved wicked people that had come out of the Millennium – because even in the Millennium people are going to be born and there's still going to be sin in the Millennium, and these people have had 1000 years to re-gather, if you will, and it's going to be Gog and Magog that are going to participate in this last battle.

VERSE 10: "And the devil that deceived them was cast into the lake of fire and brimstone, where the beast and the false prophet are, and shall be tormented day and night for ever and ever."

The false prophet and the beast, if you look carefully, never actually came up with the devil. Their fate was sealed when they fell, and it's the devil that goes back into Hell.

VERSES 11-15: "And I saw a great white throne, and him that sat on it, from whose face the earth and the heaven fled away; and there was found no place for them. And I saw the dead, small and great, stand before God; and the books were opened: and another book was opened, which is the book of life: and the dead were judged out of those things which were written in the books, according to their works. And the sea gave up the dead which were in it; and death and hell delivered up the dead which were in them: and they were judged every man according to their works. And death and hell were cast into the lake of fire. This is the second death. And whosoever was not found written in the book of life was cast into the lake of fire."

That should be quite obvious. That's your second death. Now, at the second death, according to Mark 9 verse 42, **"And whosoever shall offend one of these little ones that believe in me, it is better for him that a millstone were hanged about his neck, and he were cast into the sea. And if thy hand offend thee, cut it off: it is better for thee to enter into life maimed, than having two hands to go into hell, into** the fire that never shall be quenched: Where their worm dieth not, and the fire is not quenched. And if thy foot offend thee, cut it off: it is better for thee to enter halt into life, than having two feet to be cast into hell, into the fire that never shall be quenched: Where their worm dieth not, and the fire is not quenched. And if thine eye offend thee, pluck it out: it is better for thee to enter into the kingdom of God with one eye, than having two eyes to be cast into hell fire: Where their worm dieth not, and the fire is not quenched. For every one shall be salted with fire, and every sacrifice shall be salted with salt. Salt is good: but if the salt have lost his saltness, wherewith will ye season it? Have salt in yourselves, and have peace one with another." So at the second death, the Great White Throne has been and gone, and if you're not saved, you're going to be cast alive into the lake of fire.

Now, the question gets put, the Bible says you're going to be cast into outer darkness, according to Matthew 8, and you've got a literal fire from Revelation 20. How do we reconcile these things? Well, Luke 16:19 to 31 is the first death. I just want to go there quickly: **"And it came to pass, that the beggar died, and was carried by the angels into Abraham's bosom"** – that's a saved man dying – **"the rich man also died, and was buried."** He's just dumped in Hell. **"And in hell he lift up his eyes, being in torments, and seeth Abraham afar off, and Lazarus in his bosom. And he cried and said, Father Abraham, have mercy on me, and send Lazarus, that he may dip the tip of his finger in water, and cool my tongue; for I am tormented in this flame."** So he can speak, he can see, and he can feel. **"But Abraham said, Son, remember that thou in thy lifetime receivedst thy good things, and likewise Lazarus evil things: but now he is comforted, and thou art tormented. And beside all this, between us and you there is a great gulf fixed: so that they which would pass from hence to you cannot; neither can they pass to us, that would come from thence."** When you're dead, you're dead. You're either saved or you're lost. There's no purgatory. It's pretty bleak, period.

27: **"Then he said, I pray thee therefore, father, that thou wouldest send him to my father's house: For I have five brethren; that he may testify unto them, lest they also come into this place of torment. Abraham saith unto him, They have Moses and the prophets; let them hear them. And he said, Nay, father Abraham: but if one went unto them from the dead, they will repent. And he said unto him, If they hear not Moses and the prophets, neither will they be persuaded, though one rose from the dead."**

This man has died as he lived, as most people do, and Revelation says let him be righteous, let him be filthy still. This man knows that he's in a dreadful, awful place – and this again is the first death, not the second death. He doesn't want his family to go and join him there, and he's pleading with Abraham, who hasn't got the authority anyway to help this dead, unsaved man.

Okay. So the first death, I've just shown you that he could see, he could speak, he could feel. That's the first death. But the second death he's going to be blind, and the blindness comes from the worm which we saw in Mark 9. So picture this: You've got a person who has lost his physical features. He's going to be blind because he's in outer darkness, but he's still in a flame; he's still going to be burning in the lake of fire. So you're going to be like a maggot, in a sense, burning for all of eternity. You're going to have inner pain, inner suffering, and you're going to have people crawling all around you and on top of you like maggots do. I'm sure you've seen fishermen when they go fishing. They have all their maggots and they're put in tins, and it's just like sardines. They're all squashed on top of each other and they're all moving around. That, of course, is the second death.

And I challenge anybody who is in a church system, and if they haven't heard a sermon like this before, then I know what I would do. I wouldn't walk to the nearest door; I'd run, because this is simple

Bible. I've read nothing into the text. I haven't taken any liberties. I've exegeted the Scriptures to the best of my ability, and I've harmonised the Old Testament with the New Testament. I've used metaphorical language as and when it was needed, but I've simply given you, as far as I can see, the simplest and utmost honest exegesis of 1 to 20. And the next couple of videos we will deal with the 21st and the 22nd of Revelation.

DANIEL 12

VERSE 1: "And at that time shall Michael stand up, the great prince which standeth for the children of thy people: and there shall be a time of trouble, such as never was since there was a nation even to that same time: and at that time thy people shall be delivered, every one that shall be found written in the book."

Daniel 12 is, of course, a reference to the Great Tribulation, and we've already looked at Revelation 12 when Michael fights the devil in Heaven; and, of course, that is mirrored on the earth when Jesus is born, and we've already dealt with that bit of Scripture.

But here you have Michael standing up for the nation of Israel. The Seventh Day Adventists and the Jehovah's Witnesses have the erroneous belief that Jesus Christ is Michael the archangel. Now, Michael in Hebrew means "Who is like God?" "Jesus" translates back into the Hebrew as Joshua or Yeshua, which means "Jehovah saves." There's a difference, of course, between Michael and Jesus. Michael, being the archangel, you would find him in 1 Thessalonians Chapter 4 verse 16, and it speaks about the archangel coming with the trump of God. And a lot of people get this bit of Scripture confused, but there are two individuals here – the archangel Michael, which also fought with the devil over the body of Moses, which we've also looked at in Jude 9, but here his role is – the correct term would be "the prince of the nation of Israel."

VERSE 2: "And many of them that sleep in the dust of the earth shall awake, some to everlasting life, and some to shame and everlasting contempt."

It's quite obvious what that means. You're going to have people that have died that are going to be resurrected, and even the unsaved dead are going to be resurrected. Go to John 5. Jesus says that the Father has passed all judgment over to Him – : **"For the Father judgeth no man, but hath committed all judgment unto the Son: That all** men should honour the Son, even as they honour the Father. He that honoureth not the Son honoureth not the Father which hath sent him"; "Verily, verily, I say unto you, The hour is coming, and now is, when the dead shall hear the voice of the Son of God: and they that hear shall live"; "And hath given him authority to execute judgment also, because he is the Son of man. Marvel not at this: for the hour is coming, in the which all that are in the graves shall hear his voice." That's all without exception. "And shall come forth; they that have done good, unto the resurrection of life; and they that have done evil, unto the resurrection of damnation."

So whether you're saved or not, both Testaments affirm that there will be bodily resurrections, and at the resurrection, you are given a new body which will either take you into eternity or take you into the lake of fire, which, of course, is the second death. And we'll get to that when we reach Revelation 20.

Back to Daniel 12:3: **"And they that be wise shall shine as the brightness of the firmament; and they that turn many to righteousness as the stars for ever and ever."**

There's your soul winners. **"He that winneth souls is wise"** (Prov. 11:30.)

VERSE 4: "But thou, O Daniel, shut up the words, and seal the book, even to the time of the end: many shall run to and fro, and knowledge shall be increased."

Here Daniel is told to seal the book up, and yet John was told in Revelation that the hour, the time was now. If ever it was applicable to do Bible studies along the lines of eschatology, now is the time. Look at the Scripture here: **"Many shall run to and fro, and knowledge shall be increased."** There's absolutely no doubt that in the 21st century there's more knowledge around than ever before, and yet equally, there's a huge famine, especially in the UK. The overwhelming majority of people – and I'm thinking of young people here – in the UK have no idea about the Bible. They have no idea about the last days, the judgment, creation. They're taught evolution pretty much from day one, and it's no wonder that we have the highest abortion rate, the highest pregnancy rate, one of the highest obesity rates, and the list goes on and on and on. We have the highest list of problems, I would say, in Western Europe, and Britain has certainly forsaken her Christian heritage.

Look at 2 Timothy 3:7: **"Ever learning, and never able to come to the knowledge of the truth."** Isn't it amazing. You can have all this information and you can be reading and reading and discussing and discussing, and yet never coming to the knowledge of the truth, and, of course, the truth is found in John 14:6 – Jesus Christ, of course.

One last verse to look at on this video from Daniel, Daniel 12:10:

VERSE 10: "Many shall be purified, and made white, and tried; but the wicked shall do wickedly: and none of the wicked shall understand; but the wise shall understand."

And that really says it all, doesn't it? You've got a very small remnant of saved people in the UK at the moment, and they are surrounded by secular and agnostic fundamentalism. And the righteous know what's happening. We see the signs all around us. But if you're an evolutionist, this is the next stage of evolution, and that great gulf between the righteous and the unrighteous will quadruple and quadruple, I would say, between now and the last day.

Okay. Well, we are very nearly at the end of this impromptu series of videos on prophecy, eschatology. And I said right from the outset that I am pre-millennial and pre-tribulational, and I have been for eight years now. In fact, it was not only my father witnessing to me about ten years ago that got me very interested in the things of the Lord, but it was a book that he wrote on the Rapture and the Tribulation and, of course, into the Millennium, which really whet my appetite. And there's no doubt in my mind that Bible prophecy is one of the most important parts of Scripture. In fact, somebody once said, if you get the book Revelation straight – doctrinally, of course – everything else will fall into line. It's a bit like the book of Genesis. If you get the first eleven chapters straight and clear in your mind and you take the verses as they appear literally, then the rest of the Bible will fall into place. If you allegorise it like Augustine did and many of the church reformers also did, then you're going to miss a lot of truth when it comes to rightly dividing the word of truth.

Okay. Today I want to look at Isaiah 66 and may possibly do a couple of spin-off videos before we get back to Revelation 21.

ISAIAH 66

VERSE 1: "Thus saith the LORD, The heaven *is* my throne, and the earth *is* my footstool: where *is* the house that ye build unto me? and where *is* the place of my rest?"

Bear this in mind that the whole universe belongs to God. Therefore, He writes the rules. He can do whatever He chooses to do. He can bring in capital punishment; He can suspend it. There are a lot of people who fall into this heretical view that man is in control of this planet and God has to work with man. But that's not what the Bible says. The Scripture says it **"is my footstool,"** and this **"is the place of my rest."** And the minute we start trying to take the truth and the facts of the universe from the Lord and apply it to man, we end up deifying man and dethroning God, and that's something which we don't believe in at this ministry.

VERSE 2: "For all those things hath mine hand made – no evolution there –**"and all those things have been, saith the LORD: but to this man will I look, even to him that is poor and of a contrite spirit, and trembleth at my word."**

How many people do you know that tremble at the word of the Lord? David Brainerd was a very unusual and exceptional man of God. He was sent to the Red Indians back in the 18th century, and he had a very, very difficult ministry. And I certainly salute him, and I've even written an article about him, and I would ask you to read it, and you could learn an awful lot from this man. Yes, he was a Calvinist; yes, he would have been probably a-millennial, but nonetheless, he went out to Pennsylvania a long time ago – as I say, 300 years ago now probably – and he lived with the Red Indians. But the reason I'm mentioning him to you is because he trembled at the word of God. This man would go out in the middle of the snow, the middle of the winter and pray so intensely that the snow around him would melt. And he is a very similar person to Leonard Ravenhill, an Englishman who went to

America back in the 50s, and he used to pray in the Forest of Dean. And these two men were so passionate and also so fearful at the word of the Lord that they would spend hours in prayer before they even opened the Scripture. And, again, I wonder how many people listening to this video today would be honest enough to say that they tremble at the word of God. Look at verse 4:

VERSE 4: "I also will choose their delusions, and will bring their fears upon them; because when I called, none did answer; when I spake, they did not hear: but they did evil before mine eyes, and chose that in which I delighted not."

You have the Calvinists who believe that everything has been pre-ordained before the foundation of the world and the Lord sets out to raise up people just for the sake of destroying them. But here it says that they would not do what the Lord wanted, and therefore He will bring delusions upon them, which you'll find in 2 Thessalonians 2 and also Ephesians 4:30, I think it is, where the apostle Paul says that man gave himself up, and once he does that, then the Lord reaffirms that. The man has completely no way of coming back to be saved or be forgiven by the Lord. There does come a time when people are cut off. And I go back over history and I look at some of the Chinese Communists and dictators and Pol Pot from Cambodia and some other people from Russia, Molotov barrier – all these people. You think, "Was there ever a time when they could have been saved?" And I would say that there was a time, but sin came into their life and they never repented of it.

VERSES 5-7: "Hear the word of the LORD, ye that tremble at his word – again, there's that expression again, "tremble" – **"Your brethren that hated you, that cast you out for my name's sake, said, Let the LORD be glorified: but he shall appear to your joy, and they shall be ashamed. A voice of noise from the city, a voice from the temple, a voice of the LORD that rendereth recompence to his**

enemies. **Before she travailed, she brought forth; before her pain came, she was delivered of a man child."**

Again, the reference is to the nation of Israel, not to the Virgin Mary. And Christ came out of Israel, and you would expect Israel to be spoken of in the feminine. And nothing has changed even to this day. We speak of nations in the feminine, never the masculine.

VERSE 15: "For, behold, the LORD – capital "L," capital "O," capital "R," capital "D." This is Jehovah – **"For, behold, the LORD will come with fire, and with his chariots like a whirlwind, to render his anger with fury, and his rebuke with flames of fire."**

It hasn't happened yet, and this is not a reference to the Rapture. This is a reference to the Second Coming, Matthew 24:31.

VERSE 16: "For by fire and by his sword will the LORD plead with all flesh: and the slain of the LORD shall be many."

The word of God says that God is not willing that any should perish but that all should come to repentance (2 Pet. 3:9.) Again, Calvinists believe that is a reference to the elect and God is not willing that any of the elect would perish but all would come to repentance. Now, the problem with that is if you follow it through, Calvinism teaches that God has chosen the elect in eternity past – He came, He died just for the elect, and He's already redeemed them. Therefore, they can't fall, they can't lose their salvation. And if that would be the case, then you wouldn't have the Lord saying He doesn't want any to perish when He's already saved them. Now, I take 2 Peter 3 to be a reference to the world – God is **"not willing that any should perish, but that all should come to repentance."** Of course, men love darkness rather than light, so they're not likely to come to the light to be saved. But that doesn't mean that God doesn't want them to be saved. You won't have anybody in Hell who wasn't atoned for. Those who go to Hell go to Hell because they chose to die in their sin. And man's conscience is still very powerful, and if man would just listen to his conscience and not suppress it with drugs and alcohol and loose living, then a lot more people would be saved.

VERSE 18: "For I know their works and their thoughts: it shall come, that I will gather all nations and tongues; and they shall come, and see my glory."

It hasn't quite happened yet, but this could be a partial reference to the First Advent, but the First Advent Christ came for Israel. John 1 said He came unto His own and His own received Him not. That would have a greater fulfilment at the Second Advent.

Look at verse 8 just while we're in Isaiah still: **"Who hath heard such a thing? who hath seen such things? Shall the earth be made to bring forth in one day? or shall a nation be born at once?"** Israel was born – or reborn in modern terms in 1948, and the Bible says that He would gather all of His children from the uttermost parts of the world and bring them back, and He did that in '48. And it's interesting that America and Russia both voted to allow Israel back into the land, whereas the UK, to her shame, abstained, and it's no surprise that America and Russia became super powers almost overnight and Britain declined.

You may be wondering why it was that Russia, of all nations, voted to allow Israel to have recognition from the United Nations, and I think what Stalin was wanting to do was turn Israel into a Communist Soviet state. You see, a lot of the early Jewish leaders were Communists; they were Socialists, and Begin, of course, is one of the founders of the modern state of Israel, and Stalin was hoping that if he could get Israel to fall in line with Soviet Russia, it would give the Red Army a greater grip in the Middle East. America wasn't ignorant of this, and there was a tug-of-war for a period of years, and amazingly, the Jews sided with America, and Russia actually didn't get the grip that she wanted or the influence that she wanted over Israel. But nonetheless, both nations supported the state of Israel, and – what are we now? – 70 years on she's still in the land; she's hanging in by her fingertips, and it's not surprising by the mid forties when the Germans realised that the war was over that they turned to their Islamic friends, and the Grand Mufti was called upon to provide armies, troops, and soldiers, which Himmler happily accepted. And, of course, it wasn't to be because the Lord wanted Israel back in the land.

Okay. Back to Isaiah, Isaiah 66 verse 21: **"And I will also take of them for priests and for Levites, saith the LORD."**

I just want to stop there quickly and point out that one of the criticisms that those of us that are pre-millennial get is that by a re-implementation of the animal sacrifices this somehow negates the finished work of Christ on the cross. It doesn't because even after the Lord died and went back to glory, you had a 40-year period of the early church, believe it or not, still going up to the Temple and still partaking of the rituals. In fact, the Gospel of Luke says they went out and worshiped in the Temple daily, and Paul, by the late part of Acts, not only shaves his head but he's preparing himself to go into the Temple to take a vow. So there is this period of time, this period of dispensation when the Lord is going from the Levitical system, the priesthood and the animal sacrifice, to the full-blown period of church age.

But in the Tribulation there's going to be a third Temple, which we've already looked at in Revelation, and in the Millennium, that Temple will either be rebuilt or the one that was on the earth will remain. We're not quite sure where this additional Temple is going to come from. But look at verse 22:

VERSE 22: "For as the new heavens and the new earth, which I will make, shall remain before me, saith the LORD, so shall your seed and your name remain."

Now, once again, everything is done by the Lord and through the Lord. People are very keen to build the Kingdom of God on this earth, and sometimes they can be forgiven for wanting to do this. They want to run ahead and get everybody saved and make this a better world, and we have to be sensible and realistic that all we are told to do is to preach the Gospel and be a light to the nations. Anything beyond that would be out of our remit. And there are Christians who are very political who believe that if they get into power, they can sway governments and bring in this legislation and bring in that legislation, but you're simply tinkering with the world system. And I've said this before that when we go through the New Testament, we don't find any Scriptures, especially from Paul who had a dual nationality, we find no Scriptures about getting involved with politics trying to get this law repealed or get this law introduced. If we can get people saved from the inside, then that will reflect an outward holiness and an outward righteousness, and then people can do things individually. But to try and change the system from without, I would say it's impossible.

VERSE 23: "And it shall come to pass, that from one new moon to another, and from one sabbath to another, shall all flesh come to worship before me, saith the LORD."

Seventh Day Adventists have a real obsession with the Sabbath – and I use that word correctly and measuredly. The SDA believe that if you don't worship on a Saturday, if you don't come together for the Sabbath, that you are not only an apostate but you have received the mark of the beast; and the reality is such people are still living under Old Testament because the Sabbath wasn't only ceremonial, it wasn't only civil, but it was given as a sign from Jehovah to the Jews. And we've already looked at Galatians 3 where there's neither Greek nor Jew, bond nor free, male nor female. We are all one in Christ – positionally, of course – and that means that the Lord looks down, and when He sees His church, His redeemed, He doesn't see them as individuals but as a corporate group of people. That, of course, is in reference to when they meet to worship Him.

But here from Isaiah 66 verse 23, this is a reference to the Millennium. Now, we have a thousand years when we're going to reign on the earth, and Paul says we are going to be judging angels, and John says we will be a kingdom of priests. It's not categorically clear exactly what we will be doing or who will have what authority. Some people believe we'll have kings, angels, and dominions and cities to judge over. Others have said that we will travel space, and even those that hold to the gap theory believe that the planets, which look like they've been bombed through some war zone, are going to be re-implemented; they're going to be opened up; they're going to be given to the saints to rule from. And all that is quite possible. I wouldn't want to say it isn't.

But like I say, this is a clear reference to the Sabbath in the Millennium, not the church age. And I've already done the video on the Sabbath, and I'd like you to watch it before leaving any comments on this video about the Sabbath because it's a subject we've spent a lot of time on, and I don't want to keep going back and forward over the same subject.

VERSE 24: "And they shall go forth, and look upon the carcases of the men that have transgressed against me: for their worm shall not die, neither shall their fire be quenched; and they shall be an abhorring unto all flesh."

There is a position taken that when we are in glory we can somehow see what's going on in Hell. Now, I do believe at the first death that the picture of Abraham and Lazarus doesn't need any more explanation. I think we will be able to see what's going on. But at the second death, like I've already said, the soul of man takes on this shape of a worm, and worms are blind, so I don't think at the second death we're going to be able to see anything. Now, I do believe that at the Great White Throne, the church, the redeemed and also the Jews from the Old Testament era and the Tribulation saints, I do believe they will be there with the Lord, not judging with Him. The Mormons believe that Joseph Smith will judge the world with God the Father and God the Son. I don't think we have the audacity to claim that. But I do believe that the redeemed will be standing with the Lord.

And also keep this in mind that the Great White Throne is not for the saved man or woman to appear at. We were saved when we believed on the Lord, and we've already had our judgment, if you will, at the Judgment Seat of the Lord, and that probably occurred when we were raptured in 1 Thessalonians 4. Like I've already said, they're going to see these people that have transgressed against the Lord, and they will be abhorring unto all flesh. This also makes it crystal clear that there's no middle ground here. You can't sit on the fence. You're either with the Lord or you're against the Lord.

We meet a lot of people on the street who say, "Well, I think I'm a Christian" or "I think the Lord was a good man" or I think this or I think that, and they won't commit themselves; they won't state their case, and we need to be as clear as we can, not only in our own minds whether we actually believe on the Lord or not, but we also need to make it clear to other people. And we were told in Matthew 10 that we would confess Christ before all men, and He would then confess us before His Father and the holy angels. Again, this is elementary stuff that I'm telling you. If you are a Christian, then I'm sure most of you know this anyway. But I don't think there's any room in the church in the church age for secret-service Christians.

Just one other thing before I conclude this clip. This picture of all flesh coming to worship before the Lord, of course this is saved people. There aren't going to be unsaved people coming to the Lord. And this worship will start in the Millennium and go on into eternity because we see in verse 22 there will be a new heavens and a new earth, and that hasn't happened yet. That will occur after the thousand-year reign, and that takes us into eternity, and that's still, obviously, a future state.

Like I said at the beginning, if you get the book of Revelation straight and if you get the first eleven chapters of Genesis straight, then, God willing, everything else should fall into place. But we were told to study to show ourselves approved that we could rightly divide the word of truth. And I've said it before and I'll say it again that all of the

Bible is to us but it isn't all for us, and the more we study, the more we are faithful Bereans, the more the Lord will show us, and the more He shows us, the more we can implement what He shows us, and hopefully the more we do that, the more people will get saved and the more we can edify each other.

DANIEL 9

Okay. Daniel Chapter 9. And just before we get into the prophetic part of this book, look at Daniel 9 verse 2: **"In the first year of his reign I Daniel understood by books the number of the years, whereof the word of the LORD came to Jeremiah the prophet, that he would accomplish seventy years in the desolations of Jerusalem."**

Here we find the prophet in dire straits, and he goes to the Scripture. Now, when this account has been given to us is probably about 500 BC. Not all of the Old Testament canon was finished, and yet even with that in mind, he was able to go to Jeremiah to get an answer to his problem.

Now, we believe in this ministry in what's called Sola Scriptura, and for those that don't know, that means the Scripture alone. Tradition is no good if it hasn't got the word of God to support it, and that's one of the reasons why the Reformation took place. There was too much going on which had no scriptural authority. And we can be wrong on many things, but we cannot be wrong when it comes to the things of the Lord, and if we're teaching doctrine and we're teaching it to other people and the word of God doesn't support it, then we really are in a bad way.

Okay. From Sola Scriptura to eschatology, verse 24, 9:24:

VERSE 24: "Seventy weeks are determined upon thy people and upon thy holy city, to finish the transgression, and to make an end of sins, and to make reconciliation for iniquity, and to bring in everlasting righteousness, and to seal up the vision and prophecy, and to anoint the most Holy."

Okay. First and foremost, these 70 weeks are not literal weeks. As I say, this book was written about 550 BC, and Daniel is going to give the reader three parts of his prophecy. But first up, the reference is to **"thy people and thy holy city."** It doesn't take much to realise that Daniel is a Jew writing to the Jews about the Holy City, which, of course, is Jerusalem. Look at 25:

VERSE 25: "**Know therefore and understand, that from the going forth of the commandment to restore and to build Jerusalem unto the Messiah the Prince shall be seven weeks, and threescore and two weeks: the street shall be built again, and the wall, even in troublous times.**"

Okay. Now, the first part of this would be a reference to Ezra and Nehemiah going back and putting up the wall, but it has a much greater significance if you keep in mind that Herod's Temple was being extended in the life of the Lord Jesus Christ, and when you get to 70 AD when the Romans came to destroy it, it was still being extended. And the Wailing Wall that you see in Jerusalem today where Jews and Gentiles seem to want to go and wail at, that's actually part of Herod's wall, and Herod was a Gentile; he was an Assyrian, I believe.

VERSE 26: "**And after threescore and two weeks shall Messiah be cut off, but not for himself:**" –

Now, you all know, if you've ever looked at church history and even secular history, that the Messiah didn't die for anything He had done. In fact, He says in Scripture, "**Which of you convinceth me of sin?**" And nobody said a word. There was opportunity. They'd been murmuring; they'd been backbiting; they'd been doing all sorts of things behind the Lord's back, and He gives them the opportunity to come out in His presence and state their feelings about Him, and nobody said a word. And we've done this in other videos. You look at anybody else – let's look at Buddha very quickly. Here's a man that came from royalty, and one day he believed he had a vision or had some light from a higher force, and he left his family, deserted them and went off with his higher light. Confucius, an ancient mystic – again, these are both pre-Christ – and the man would get drunk from time to time. Just a couple of ancient people from antiquity, and you wouldn't be able to say with a straight face that they were without sin.

But Daniel says that Messiah would be cut off **"but not for himself:"** – Look at this – colon – **"and the people of the prince that shall come shall destroy the city and the sanctuary;"**

I just want to hold it there. On a few videos ago I showed you in Acts Chapter 2 when just a colon or a semicolon can separate two periods of time. And if you don't read the Scriptures carefully, you'd miss it. Also keep in mind that in the 'original Greek' and the 'original Hebrew,' there is no grammar; there's no false starts or commas or semicolons. It's all upper case, especially in the Greek. So you wouldn't notice this if you're going through the Greek. But we're in the Old Testament here which, of course, was penned in Hebrew, and you can see this quite clearly in the English. Let's look at it one more time:

"And after threescore and two weeks shall Messiah be cut off, but not for himself:" – colon – **"and the people of the prince"** – So, you see, there's two periods here. Jesus dies in around April 30 AD, and then the text goes on – **"and the people of the prince that shall come shall destroy the city"** – which would be Jerusalem – **"and the sanctuary;"** – the Holy of Holies – **"and the end thereof shall be with a flood"** – again, that's Second Advent. We looked at that in Revelation 12 – **"and unto the end of the war desolations are determined."**

So you've got the first coming in 30 AD; you've got a partial reference to 70 AD – and that will please the Preterists – and you've got a greater reference to the Second Coming, the flood. And I've said this before, when you read the Scripture, read it very carefully, and above all, tremble because you're dealing with the word of God here.

VERSE 27: **"And he"** – Who's "he"? It's the Antichrist, of course, the prince which we've just seen in 26 – **"And he shall confirm the covenant with many for one week: and in the midst of the week he shall cause the sacrifice and the oblation to cease, and for the overspreading of abominations he shall make it desolate, even until**

the consummation, and that determined shall be poured upon the desolate."

Okay. Let's break this down. The Antichrist is going to confirm a covenant with many for one week, and in the middle of that one week, he's going to cause the sacrifice to cease. Again, this isn't a reference to seven days. This week will be found probably in the second part of the Great Tribulation, and the oblation, which is a reference to the daily sacrifices, are going to be stopped. We know in the Tribulation there will be a third Temple, and the Jews will be going about their business. They've got their own priesthood; they've got their own garments; they've got the drawings. They're all ready to go now. But the political will from Tel Aviv isn't yet matched in the political realm. To put a Temple up even in these days would still be very risky. But we know in the Tribulation that the Temple will go up, and once that goes up, then we really are ticking down to the Second Advent.

The Jews will be busy in the Temple, as I say, but the Antichrist is going to break this false peace. And we've said it so many times before that when you've got people around the world trying to force a peace on little old secular Israel, little old democracy Israel, little old 7 million-strong Israel, nothing will come of it. The Peace Quartet will come and go, the Oslo talks came and went, and no matter what Secretary of State you've got in the White House or what President you've got in the Oval Office or whoever is running the European Union – and, of course, they play a part in Bible prophecy too – no matter who you've got and what they're doing, nothing is going to come to pass. And even with the Antichrist on the scene, all of the left-wing, atheist, peace-loving organisations are going to throw their lot in with him, and nothing that he does or touches will in any way come to pass.

Revelation again

CHAPTER 21 VERSE 1: "And I saw a new heaven and a new earth: for the first heaven and the first earth were passed away; and there was no more sea."

Go to 2 Peter Chapter 3 verse 3: **"Knowing this first, that there shall come in the last days scoffers, walking after their own lusts, And saying, Where is the promise of his coming? for since the fathers fell asleep, all things continue as they were from the beginning of the creation. For this they willingly are ignorant of, that by the word of God the heavens were of old, and the earth standing out of the water and in the water: Whereby the world that then was, being overflowed with water, perished: But the heavens and the earth, which are now, by the same word are kept in store, reserved unto fire against the day of judgment and perdition of ungodly men."**

Ten: **"But the day of the Lord will come as a thief in the night; in the which the heavens shall pass away with a great noise, and the elements shall melt with fervent heat, the earth also and the works that are therein shall be burned up."** Here is your big bang theory, and we haven't had that yet, of course. This is still a future reference.

Eleven: **"Seeing then that all these things shall be dissolved, what manner of persons ought ye to be in all holy conversation and godliness, Looking for and hasting unto the coming of the day of God, wherein the heavens being on fire shall be dissolved, and the elements shall melt with fervent heat?"**

Now, this is obviously still a future account of what's going to come at the end of the Tribulation, at the end of the thousand-year reign.

VERSES 2-3: "And I John saw the holy city, new Jerusalem, coming down from God out of heaven, prepared as a bride adorned for her husband. And I heard a great voice out of heaven saying, Behold, the tabernacle of God is with men, and he will dwell with them, and they shall be his people, and God himself shall be with them, and be their God."

Now, the New Jerusalem, of course, is going to be the eternal abode for the redeemed. All of your church age and Old Testament age and Tribulation age and all those saved in the Millennium are going to go into the New Jerusalem, and some people think it will hover over the earth, and some people believe it will actually come to the new earth. But nonetheless, it will be, I think, 1400 miles in diameter. And we'll get to that in a minute.

VERSE 4: "And God shall wipe away all tears from their eyes; and there shall be no more death, neither sorrow, nor crying, neither shall there be any more pain: for the former things are passed away."

It should be quite obvious to say that once we are redeemed and glorified, all of our past memories and all of our failures and all of the things that made us sad and anything that was distracting us and all our physical and mental and psychological and any illness or disability which we may have had or still have will be completely done away. We are a new creation in Christ Jesus.

VERSES 5-6: "And he that sat upon the throne said, Behold, I make all things new. And he said unto me, Write: for these words are true and faithful. And he said unto me, It is done. I am Alpha and Omega, the beginning and the end. I will give unto him that is athirst of the fountain of the water of life freely."

Just keep this in mind that back in Genesis Chapter 1 the Lord spoke everything into existence – the triune God, of course – and one of the problems we have with the Apostles' Creed and the Nicene Creed as well is that it says that we believe in one God, the Father of all, Creator of Heaven and earth, which is fine, but it negates the fact that the Son of God was also part of the creation as was the Holy Spirit. And we don't accept that Creed because we don't think it reflects the triunity of God.

But here you've got the Son of God, the Alpha and the Omega, sitting on the throne, and He's going to make all things new. Again,

Jesus Christ is very God and very man, and Paul told us in 1 Timothy that He was God manifest in the flesh, and He's going to give of the fountain of water of life freely.

VERSE 7: "He that overcometh shall inherit all things; and I will be his God, and he shall be my son."

And we've already looked at 1 John Chapter 5 that you overcome the world and you become an overcomer by your faith in the Lord Jesus Christ.

VERSE 8: "But the fearful, and unbelieving, and the abominable, and murderers, and whoremongers, and sorcerers, and idolaters, and all liars, shall have their part in the lake which burneth with fire and brimstone: which is the second death."

Now, we've already looked at the lake of fire from 19:20, and it wasn't just the beast and the false prophet that went in there; it's also going to be liars, murderers, whoremongers, sorcerers, and idolaters. And 1 John 3:15 says that if you hate your brother – and that would be a reference to another Christian – you would be a murderer if you hate. Just the hate alone will put you into Hell, and, of course, John also says that those that hate their brothers don't have eternal life abiding in them. So if you know a Christian that hates another Christian – and I mean hates another Christian, not just dislikes but hates another Christian and is out to maybe smear that Christian or destroy that Christian's integrity or testimony or whatever – then you're dealing with an unsaved person according to 1 John 3, and his fate, according to Revelation 21:8, is in the lake of fire.

Idolaters are not just people who worship statues or have their rosary beads or worship church buildings or a chalice or what have you; it can be a person who worships their family, worships their ministry, worships their cars, the women in their life. It can be a hundred and one things, and if you don't repent of that idolatry, then it says here you'll go into the lake of fire.

VERSES 9-10: "And there came unto me one of the seven angels which had the seven vials full of the seven last plagues, and talked with me, saying, Come hither, I will shew thee the bride, the Lamb's wife. And he carried me away in the spirit to a great and high mountain, and shewed me that great city, the holy Jerusalem, descending out of heaven from God,"

It's obvious that at the present time the New Jerusalem hasn't been built, but once it is built, it will come down from Heaven. That much we can say for sure.

VERSES 11-12: "Having the glory of God: and her light was like unto a stone most precious, even like a jasper stone, clear as crystal; And had a wall great and high, and had twelve gates, and at the gates twelve angels, and names written thereon, which are the names of the twelve tribes of the children of Israel:"

Time and time again you will see this is a Jewish book. Again, the Jews are the apple of God's eye, and it's the church which is grafted into the Jewish root. Anything that we have as Gentiles is simply by the grace of God. Had the Jews received Christ at the First Advent, then there's every possibility you wouldn't have had 2,000 years of church age. Christ was ready to come back in the early chapters of the book of Acts, but they didn't receive Him; they rejected Him as the Old Testament prophets said would happen, and therefore, Paul says we now switch from the Jews and we go to the Gentiles. And, of course, that was all in the mind of the Lord, of course; but, nonetheless, the option was given to the Jewish people in the 30s and the 40s and the 50s in the first century whether to receive en masse or reject en masse, and unfortunately for them, they rejected the Lord, but fortunately for us, we got grafted in.

VERSE 14: "And the wall of the city had twelve foundations, and in them the names of the twelve apostles of the Lamb."

Now, when you get to the naming and the numbering of the apostles, it gets a bit tricky because Judas died, which left us eleven apostles. But a lot of the scholars that I've read since I became a Christian have said that had the apostles waited until Acts Chapter 9, then Paul would have come and he would have replaced Judas, which sounds a bit of a poison chalice, but it would have put the apostles back at twelve – again, twelve tribes of Israel, the twelve sons of Jacob, and the twelve apostles. But nonetheless, I would say that Paul would be the twelfth apostle, and Matthias would probably be given an honorary part or an honorary role to play in the future Eternal City.

VERSES 16-18: "And the city lieth foursquare, and the length is as large as the breadth: and he measured the city with the reed, twelve thousand furlongs. The length and the breadth and the height of it are equal. And he measured the wall thereof, an hundred and forty and four cubits, according to the measure of a man, that is, of the angel. And the building of the wall of it was of jasper: and the city was pure gold, like unto clear glass."

And 19, 20, 21 will give you more information about the pearls and the gates and the beauty which awaits those that are redeemed.

VERSE 22: "And I saw no temple therein: for the Lord God Almighty and the Lamb are the temple of it."

Two things to say. First of all, from the Old Testament right up till Herod's Temple, the Jews had a Temple. Of course, Solomon's Temple was destroyed, and in the Tribulation, the Temple will be built again. Paul told us in 1 Corinthians 3 and 6 that the Christian – singular – was the temple of God, but here in the Eternal City going into eternity, the Lord God and the Lamb are going to be the Temple.

VERSES 23-24: "And the city had no need of the sun, neither of the moon, to shine in it: for the glory of God did lighten it, and the Lamb is the light thereof. And the nations of them which are saved shall walk in the light of it: and the kings of the earth do bring their glory and honour into it."

Okay. This is an interesting Scripture, verse 24. And I was looking at some of the Bible commentaries I've got on this final part of

Revelation. In fact, this final part of Revelation has been probably the hardest for me to get clear in my own mind to then do a video on it. I've read books over the years on Revelation and Bible prophecy in general, but like most Christians – I'm sure that you would agree with me – I'd rather find these things myself, and this reference in 24 says the nations which are saved shall walk in them. We know that we are called a peculiar nation, a peculiar people, and the Lord said that the Kingdom would be taken from one nation and given to another. So the reference here, "nations," is going to be peoples, and, of course, peoples make up nations. And Matthew 25, you get the goats and the sheep, and the sheep become a people and they go into the Millennium. And we know in the Millennium that there will be children born, not from the church age or the Old Testament Jews but people that have lived at the end of the Tribulation that have survived the Antichrist. They got saved and they weren't put to death, and it will be those people that go into the Millennium to re-populate it.

So this expression "the nations," I would understand that to be a reference to the saved people, and there's also kings of the earth which also get in on the action. But like I said in a previous video, Revelation 1 speaks about us being a kingdom of priests, so I'm not sure we can stretch it any more than that.

I want to say one other thing quickly. The First Advent, the wise men came to the Lord with gifts, and that's going to be reflected in the Second Advent. And they were considered to be kings, Magi, by many in their generation. And I remember somebody asking a well-known Bible scholar what happened to the gifts that they gave to Mary and Joseph and the Lord Jesus, of course, and the response was they probably gave them to the Temple, and that's quite possible if not probable, I would say.

VERSE 25: "And the gates of it shall not be shut at all by day: for there shall be no night there."

And also they won't need to be closed because nothing unclean is going to enter in.

VERSES 26-27: "And they shall bring the glory and honour of the nations into it. And there shall in no wise enter into it any thing that defileth, neither whatsoever worketh abomination, or maketh a lie: but they which are written in the Lamb's book of life."

Again, it's quite obvious that by this stage you've had the Great White Throne; you've had the Judgment Seat for the saved people, and we are now perfectly and sinlessly into eternity. And next up we'll look at the 22nd chapter.

CHAPTER 22

VERSES 1-2: "And he shewed me a pure river of water of life, clear as crystal, proceeding out of the throne of God and of the Lamb. In the midst of the street of it, and on either side of the river, was there the tree of life, which bare twelve manner of fruits, and yielded her fruit every month: and the leaves of the tree were for the healing of the nations."

I just want to stop there and point out that in the book of Genesis we have at least three trees in the Garden of Eden, and the Lord said to Adam and Eve two trees you can eat from but the third tree you can't eat from. Now, there may have been more trees, but the point is that out of the three trees that are mentioned, one is out of bounds. And so many people, agnostics and atheists and so on and so forth, have made such a noise over the years over this part of Scripture, and some have had the audacity to suggest the Lord was tricking Adam and Eve. But we have to remember that the Lord sets the rules. This is His universe. And if you're a child, you do as your parents tell you; if you're an employee, you do as your boss tells you; and if you're a member of society, you do what the State tells you. It goes right up to the top, and in the UK, the Prime Minister has to report to the Queen at least once a week. Even in America the President has to work in harmony with both houses of congress.

So this picture of the Lord having complete control and setting the rules shouldn't be unheard of. In fact, I'm going to list in the description box an article which I came across some years ago called *"The Suffering Saviour."* It was written back in the 60s by an unknown author. It's a very interesting write-up. But when you get a chance read it, and I think before you pass judgment on the Lord of the Bible, you may want to just read this and think again.

But just one other quick point. We know that Eve listened to the devil, and, of course, he tricked her into eating of the fruit, and it's quite possible that wasn't the first time that the devil had spoken to her. And once she fell into sin, then her husband followed her and they both fell into sin. And, of course, if you read the text in Genesis 3, the Lord comes into the Garden in the heat of the day and He confronts Adam, first of all, and He said, "What have you done?" And he blames the Lord. He says, "It's all your fault, Lord. The woman you gave me, she made me do it." Then He confronts Eve, and she said, "Well, it was the devil's fault; he made me do it." And here's a typical picture of people not taking responsibility for their actions. We've looked at Nuremberg back in the forties when the Nazis were tried for their war crimes, and one after the other, they all tried to pass the buck – "Well, we were just following orders," and, of course, that set a precedent at the Nuremberg that from now on, such an excuse wouldn't wash.

But as I say, Adam and Eve didn't want to take responsibility, and the Lord punished Adam, and He said from now on, man will have to work and it's not going to be an easy ride, and women will suffer in childbirth. There's always consequences of sin, no matter who you are, what you are, and the word of God says, **"Be sure your sin will find you out"** (Num. 32:23.)

Just one other thing. The nations that we see in verse 2 would be a reference to the same nations from 21:24, which I would believe would be a reference to the saved people, the saved sheep that have gone into the Millennium after the judgment from Matthew 25.

VERSE 3: "And there shall be no more curse: but the throne of God and of the Lamb shall be in it; and his servants shall serve him:"

Again, that curse goes back to the fall of man. And it wasn't just men or mankind that fell; it also affected the whole planet. No doubt there's thunderstorms and tidal waves, and even the animal kingdom suffered in the fall of man. Also, if you read Galatians 3, it says that Christ became a curse for us.

VERSES 4-6: "And they shall see his face; and his name shall be in their foreheads. And there shall be no night there; and they need no candle, neither light of the sun; for the Lord God giveth them light: and they shall reign for ever and ever. And he said unto me, These sayings are faithful and true: and the Lord God of the holy prophets sent his angel to shew unto his servants the things which must shortly be done."

Again, that expression **"shortly be done"** doesn't necessarily mean it's going to happen in the next few minutes, but it does have an essence of imminency – a bit like the Rapture. The Rapture could happen at any moment. We don't know. But we were told to be holy, for God is holy, and we don't want to be caught in iniquity if the Rapture should come in the next few moments.

VERSE 7: "Behold, I come quickly: blessed is he that keepeth the sayings of the prophecy of this book."

And that's a throwback to the first Chapter of Revelation. This is the only book in the Bible which promises a blessing to its reader, and how tragic it is that so many people completely ignore this book, and those that do read it end up spiritualising it; and that's to their loss because the great soul winners of the past 4-500 years have nearly all been pre-millennial, and they've taken this book seriously and they've given it the respect that it deserves.

VERSE 8: "And I John saw these things, and heard them. And when I had heard and seen, I fell down to worship before the feet of the angel which shewed me these things."

Again, you don't worship anybody or anything but the Lord God.

VERSE 9: "Then saith he unto me, See thou do it not: for I am thy fellowservant, and of thy brethren the prophets, and of them which keep the sayings of this book: worship God."

An angel, of all people, is identifying himself with flesh and blood. Again, that's humility.

VERSE 10: "And he saith unto me, Seal not the sayings of the prophecy of this book: for the time is at hand."

Now, Daniel was told in 500 BC to seal the book, seal his prophetic visions because at that time, it wasn't relevant. But here John on the Isle of Patmos around 90-something AD under the Emperor Domitian has been told not to seal up the prophecy. Now, look at 11:

VERSE 11: "He that is unjust, let him be unjust still: and he which is filthy, let him be filthy still: and he that is righteous, let him be righteous still: and he that is holy, let him be holy still."

In other words, whatever position you are, if you're not going to bend the knee and confess Christ as Lord, then you simply remain as you are and you'll die as you live and you'll retain your fallen nature. And, again, Luke 16 is not a parable. It's a clear expression of a person who died before the death, burial, and resurrection of the Lord Jesus Christ, and even then it was pretty horrific to read of what that first, not the second but what the first death entailed.

VERSE 12: "And, behold, I come quickly; and my reward is with me, to give every man according as his work shall be."

Again, we're going to be given rewards if we were faithful. And, again, our salvation does not depend on our works. We're not working to be saved and we're not working to stay saved. We do works because we are saved, and Ephesians 2 says we would be saved unto good works. And people get James 2 and Romans 4 muddled up, and they force the

Bible to teach faith and works, which is nonsense. If you read Romans 4 carefully, the context is about faith before God. Again, God looks at the heart; man looks on the outward appearance, whereas James is talking about your faith in front of men. Abraham was going to offer Isaac as an offering, and he had a couple of servants with him, and that reflected his faith, if you will. And he didn't kill him, obviously. The Lord stopped him. But his heart was obviously circumcised, and the Lord saw his heart which generated the works which were seen by his servants. So there's no reason to get James 2 and Romans 4 muddled up.

VERSE 14: "Blessed are they that do his commandments, that they may have right to the tree of life, and may enter in through the gates into the city."

Now, we've already looked at these commandments which we found in 1 John Chapter 3, and even Paul talks about the commandments in 1 Corinthians 7. So we don't need to change the text here, which a lot of new Bibles have done. We can leave it as it stands and understand these commandments are to believe on the Lord Jesus Christ and to love your brother as yourself.

VERSE 15: "For without" – for outside – **"For without are dogs, and sorcerers, and whoremongers, and murderers, and idolaters, and whosoever loveth and maketh a lie."**

Again, that would be a reference to the lake of fire which is eternal.

VERSES 16-17: "I Jesus have sent mine angel to testify unto you these things in the churches. I am the root and the offspring of David, and the bright and morning star. And the Spirit and the bride say, Come. And let him that heareth say, Come. And let him that is athirst come. And whosoever will, let him take the water of life freely."

Again, the Lord is not willing that any should perish but that all should come to repentance. Why don't you come to the Lord today. Get on your knees and call out to Him.

VERSES 18-20: "For I testify unto every man that heareth the words of the prophecy of this book, If any man shall add unto these things, God shall add unto him the plagues that are written in this book: And if any man shall take away from the words of the book of this prophecy, God shall take away his part out of the book of life, and out of the holy city, and from the things which are written in this book. He which testifieth these things saith, Surely I come quickly. Amen. Even so, come, Lord Jesus."

And that should be the prayer of everybody who is born again that we want to see the Lord come today if possible. And there's a picture of the Rapture, an imminent Rapture. We can't say when, but it could be imminent.

VERSE 21: "The grace of our Lord Jesus Christ be with you all. Amen."

And that concludes this impromptu series of clips on the book of Revelation. It's a fascinating book, and if you haven't read it all the way through, please read it. Take your time with it. And it normally takes me about three and a half hours to read it all the way through, and that's reading it with fear and reverence, if you will, because of so much in this book. And if you're one of those people who have read it and you've studied it for many years, then let me know what you think about it.

But this is the word of God. This is the Scripture, and this has every reason to be in the canon of Scripture. And, as I say, it was a big part of my life when I first became a Christian realising that prophecy was so prominent in the word of God and so neglected at the same time, and I'm just thankful that the Lord has given me a hunger for His word and to understand just how the last days are going to play out.

Also by James Battell

The Shocking History of the Jesuits (The Society of Jesus)
King James I of England: The King The Vatican Could Not Kill
The Hidden Truth About Freemasonry, The Catholic Church, And
The Illuminati
Bible Prophecy Made Simple For Serious Students of Scripture
Did The Catholic Church Order Abraham Lincoln's Assassination?
Is Calvinism and the Doctrines of Grace Biblical?
The Book of Genesis Commentary (Chapters 1-11)
The Book of Genesis Commentary (Chapters 1-11)
Watchman Nee, Witness Lee, and Living Stream Ministry: A Critical
Analysis of Their Identity as Cult or Church
What Is Speaking In Tongues And Is It Still For Today?
Ephesians KJV Bible Commentary
The Book of Romans Commentary
Philemon Bible Study (Slavery In Scripture)
Turbulent Thrones: Charles vs. Cromwell's Epic Struggle for England's
Soul
The Holy Ghost Within The Trinity
Papal Infallibility or Insanity?
The Immaculate Conception ("Deception")